THE *River Cottage*

AUSTRALIA COOKBOOK

PAUL WEST

Foreword by
HUGH FEARNLEY-WHITTINGSTALL

PHOTOGRAPHY BY MARK CHEW
ILLUSTRATIONS BY KAT CHADWICK

B L O O M S B U R Y
LONDON · NEW DELHI · NEW YORK · SYDNEY

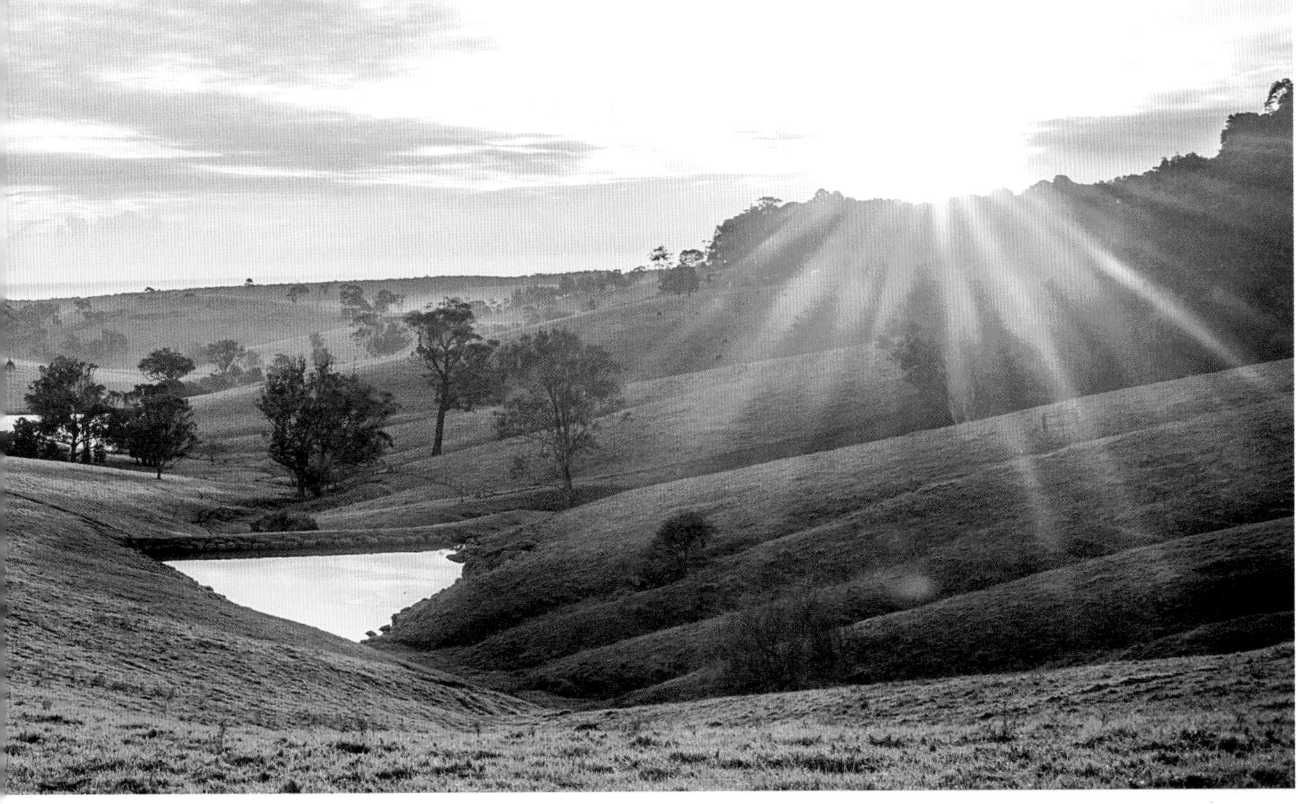

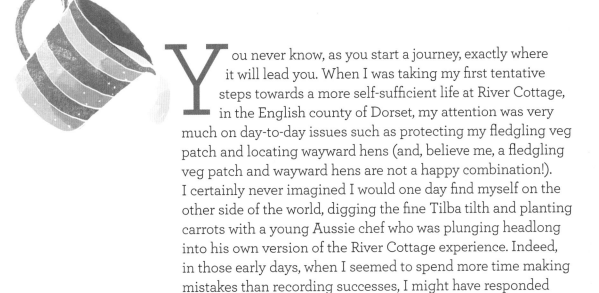

You never know, as you start a journey, exactly where it will lead you. When I was taking my first tentative steps towards a more self-sufficient life at River Cottage, in the English county of Dorset, my attention was very much on day-to-day issues such as protecting my fledgling veg patch and locating wayward hens (and, believe me, a fledgling veg patch and wayward hens are not a happy combination!). I certainly never imagined I would one day find myself on the other side of the world, digging the fine Tilba tilth and planting carrots with a young Aussie chef who was plunging headlong into his own version of the River Cottage experience. Indeed, in those early days, when I seemed to spend more time making mistakes than recording successes, I might have responded to the idea of anyone wanting to tread a similar path with a sardonic laugh.

And yet, fifteen years on from my first forays into producing my own food, the spirit of those endeavours has flourished and, indeed, travelled. I'd be lying if I said I wasn't rather proud.

From the outset, though, I've known I'm not alone in wanting a better, more fulfilling relationship with food. The success of the River Cottage enterprise is in no small part down to a groundswell of feeling that I was able to tap into. From day one, I was constantly meeting people who shared my desire to eat tasty, well-produced local fare and to avoid the processed, the machine-made and the unseasonal. And that's just as true today: there are countless individuals who feel disillusioned with modern food-production – and if you're reading this book, I'd guess there's a more than reasonable chance that you're one of them. Welcome!

My decision to move to the country in 1999 was inspired by an urge to cut out the middle man, to get back to the source of the fruit, veg, meat and bread I put in my shopping basket – and, wherever possible, to lose the shopping basket altogether. As an avowed foodie – both a restaurant critic and a chef – I was feeling an increasing sense of dislocation from the food I was eating. It wasn't just that so much of what was on offer was of poor quality, but also that a lot of it was also somehow mysterious – or at least raised some troubling questions. What were all those additives? Why did so many vegetables look like they'd been steam-cleaned and polished? How come the supermarket shelves were so overloaded with chicken breasts – where was the rest of the bird?

I didn't want to simply answer these questions – I wanted to go beyond them, to get to grips with what I was eating, so to speak. And I couldn't think of a better way to do that than to start producing some of it myself. I wasn't a total novice – I had fond memories of my Dad's vegetable garden and the lovely dishes my Mum would cook with the harvest that came from it; I knew what fresh food ought to look like, smell like and taste like. But still, it was a big step to actually roll up my sleeves and start digging. Why? Because our society, our food culture, is increasingly geared away from people actually having anything to do with the things they put on their plates. In order to reconnect with my food and drink, a complete step-change was in order.

Growing, gathering and raising my own food has brought me huge satisfaction, not to mention many delicious meals. There are few things more wonderful than feeding your family with something you have not just cooked but produced yourself. I've got to say that, as I dug deep into the issues surrounding our modern-day diet, I uncovered some very disturbing truths – so much so that I was compelled to take action. River Cottage campaigns including Chicken Out! and Hugh's Fish Fight have grown out of the knowledge that some of our food is produced and harvested in truly shocking ways. However, the depressing facts have always been balanced by the uplifting ones. For every sad and sorry story of factory farming or dubious ingredients I've come across, I've discovered something inspiring and hopeful: local people

joining together to share land and raise food, a huge proliferation in organic box schemes and farmers' markets, schools where the kids grow their own veg, campaigners who refuse to be silenced and many, many producers of really wonderful ingredients.

If, like me and like Paul West, you want to resist the pull towards mass-produced factory fare, you needn't up sticks and move to a remote outpost, or chuck in the day job and start buying piglets – though of course I'd heartily applaud such commitment! But in fact, you don't have to move an inch from where you are now in order to start feeling happier about the food you buy, cook and eat. We all have the option of doing things differently, no matter where we live, what we do or how much we earn.

Early on in my River Cottage venture I developed the idea of a 'food acquisition continuum'. This is just a fancy way of describing the spectrum we're all on with regard to where our food comes from. At one end of the continuum (the far right, if you like) is complete dependence on industrialised producers and big retailers, and at the opposite end (let's call it the far left), total self-sufficiency. Wherever you are on this continuum, I firmly believe that any shift towards the left, however slight, is a move in the right direction.

Such a shift might be signalled by something as simple as buying your eggs from a neighbour with free-range hens, or visiting a pick-your-own farm in strawberry season. It might mean growing a few pots of herbs on your windowsill or baking a loaf of your own bread now and then. Any small decision of this kind is significant – it's profound, in fact, because it means you are wresting back a little bit of control over your own nourishment and nutrition.

And small steps often lead to larger ones. Choosing to eat or shop in a more positive and sustainable way almost inevitably results in a sense of satisfaction and achievement that will encourage you to make more changes. You might even find yourself keeping a couple of chooks in your own backyard, or planting a fruit tree; maybe growing some veg or blowing the cobwebs off that fishing rod in the attic. In my experience, all these things will bring you a far greater understanding of your food, and a deeper pleasure when you come to tuck into it. They'll make you a better cook and a wiser eater – and that's got to make for a more fulfilling life.

I know Paul agrees, because he walks the talk every day, in his kitchen, garden and paddocks at River Cottage Australia. In him, I've found a fantastic colleague and a trusted new friend (or mate, perhaps I should say). Paul shares the pioneering spirit I hope I exhibited when I set out on my River Cottage undertaking and he has all the good humour and adaptability essential to anyone launching themselves into the project of self-sufficiency.

Paul certainly knows his food – he's a wonderful, natural chef. His learning curve when it came to producing that food himself was steep, just as mine was, but it's been a joy to watch him get to grips with everything from hen-house building and seed-sowing to bartering and water management. I know that anyone who has watched the River Cottage Australia series will have learnt a huge amount from his endeavours.

With this book, you'll learn a lot more. It will, I believe, spur you on to begin a River Cottage–style adventure of your own, whether via small changes or big ones. Everything I've done at River Cottage in England and all that Paul has worked for in his beautiful corner of Australia is inspired by the same fervent belief: that our food should be a source of pleasure and good health and that we should feel great about every mouthful. The good news is that such a goal is within everyone's reach and the even better news is that getting closer to it involves no hardship or sacrifice. On the contrary, it will bring you great enjoyment and tangible rewards.

The joy of this journey is that it continues – I'm certainly still learning, trying out new things and developing different ways to make the most of the ingredients I grow, gather and buy. I know Paul is too, and anyone who is striving towards a more holistic and rewarding way of eating will tell you there's always more to discover. But I reckon I can promise you this: taking even a small step in the River Cottage direction is something you'll never regret.

HUGH FEARNLEY-WHITTINGSTALL, MARCH 2015

Food is a fundamental part of our everyday life. We need it to live, to grow and to fuel our bodies for the amazing adventure that is life. At its most basic level, food is just something that we put in our mouths, chew and absorb into our systems. However, looking at food in this simplistic manner fails to do justice to a ritual that can be a truly magical experience. Nothing else engages all the senses in the same way as sitting down to a well-cooked, nutritious meal with a group of family or friends. Food not only fuels our bodies, but also our souls; no matter what the culture, cuisine or ingredients, sitting down to share a meal with family and friends is something that unites us all.

Food is something that I live and breathe but it hasn't always been that way. I don't come from a long line of culinary adventurers, my family aren't farmers and for a long time, my greatest culinary achievement was to spread Vegemite on toast. My childhood home was very much of the meat-and-three-veg variety and while I'm eternally grateful to Mum for putting a hearty feed on the table every night, I wasn't really interested in what was on my plate. I didn't play any part in feeding myself other than using a knife and fork, chewing and swallowing. It wasn't until I left home and started to fend for myself that I realised what a huge part food could play in your life.

When I was twenty-one I embarked on a solo hitchhiking adventure around Australia. It was on this journey that I was introduced to a way of life that I had no idea existed. I was in northern Tasmania and had been travelling by myself for around three months when something happened that would change my life forever. Fed up with camping and staying at hostels, and desperate for a home-cooked meal, I signed up to the organisation Willing Workers On Organic Farms (WWOOF). For those who've never heard of wwoofing, the idea is that organic farms offer to take on wwoofers, feeding and accommodating them in exchange for four hours' work a day. I called up a farm that was about an hour away from where I was staying. The farmer was a retired French carpenter called Giles and his farm was in an area with the rather promising name of Paradise. Arriving late in the evening on my first day, I was introduced to the family, fed a light supper and then shown to my quarters. Giles told me to get a good night's sleep and that he'd come and get me in the morning for breakfast.

The next day Giles banged on my door at 5am to inform me breakfast was ready and that I must pick some apples and pears from the orchard to juice. I groaned as I got out of bed, dressed, put my boots on and stumbled, bleary-eyed, into the grey, pre-dawn orchard. It was late March so the trees were absolutely laden with dew-covered fruit. I picked as many as I could carry and couldn't help but bite into one of the pears. To this day I've never tasted a piece of fruit that can come close to that pear. I hadn't eaten fruit straight off the tree before and after that first taste I was hooked. I made my way to the farmhouse where Giles had prepared a steaming pot of porridge on the wood-fired stove, using milk from his neighbour's dairy. To top it all off, Giles pulled out of the oven a loaf of freshly baked bread that we would enjoy for lunch with veggies from the garden. My head was spinning – all this amazing, simple food was knocking my socks off. In one morning my whole perception of food and what it could be had changed. I had just witnessed the good life and I was determined to make it my own.

The only thing holding me back was a total lack of skills. I couldn't garden and I couldn't cook to save myself. Luckily time was on my side so I set out to teach myself everything that I would need to know about growing food and cooking it so that one day I could live in my own little slice of paradise. First off, I learnt to grow things. I continued my wwoofing journey around Australia, gleaning little bits of farming and gardening knowledge at every farm that I visited. After I returned home to the Hunter Valley, I continued my green thumb apprenticeship by volunteering for local permaculture groups and community gardens. It was while working with

these groups that I witnessed the power of growing food as a community. I realised the way it could bring together people from all kinds of different backgrounds to share in a common joy, and the way that ideas and knowledge were freely shared between people. It made me realise that I didn't want to work towards being self-sufficient, I wanted to be a part of a community that shared the same values as me when it came to food.

By this stage I was pretty confident that I could grow things to eat. By no means was I a master gardener but I had certainly come a long way. Cooking, on the other hand, was an entirely different story. I clearly remember my culinary low point. I was still in my early twenties and strapped for cash. I wanted to cook something that was hearty and cheap and I thought fried rice wouldn't be too difficult to whip up. It sounded straightforward. How hard could it be to fry rice? I bought a pack of rice and a few other bits and bobs to go with it and set to work. I heated up a frypan, added a little oil and then poured in a couple of cups of uncooked rice. I stirred and stirred, turned the heat up and then down again, added more oil, but the rice just wouldn't cook. You can laugh – it's ok, that's what my friends, who were all capable cooks, did when they came home and caught me in this act of culinary neophytism. My failed fried rice was a sign that I was severely lacking in the kitchen skills department, so I did what no rational person would and took on a chef's apprenticeship.

I got my start working for a mate at a nice enough café on the local strip. I did more dishes than cooking for the first couple of months but I was already learning the basics. Over the next couple of years I chased progressively more prestigious kitchens until eventually I found myself shaking the pans at a fancy fine diner in Melbourne. Here I learnt a lot about food and myself. I was shown how to butcher, fillet, dice *very* finely, make sauces and soufflés and how to put food beautifully onto a plate. I also discovered that I could work ninety hours a week, barely see the sun and survive on a diet of adrenaline, coffee and cigarettes. I found that you could cook hundreds of meals a day and never sit down to enjoy one yourself, and that when people pay for food at a flash restaurant they often spend more time looking for flaws than enjoying the meal. I realised that I had become so preoccupied with becoming a better cook that I had totally forgotten why I wanted to cook in the first place. After two years in that stainless steel tank, I resigned and reassessed where I was headed.

After a bit of soul-searching I decided to pack up and move to Tasmania, back to the state where it all began. My partner and I both took jobs working for a restaurant where the owners genuinely cared for their staff and about the provenance of everything they put on the menu. We put a deposit on a little place in a coastal village about forty-five minutes out of Hobart and I set to work turning the yard into a food-producing paradise. I bought my first chickens, collected my first home-grown eggs, planted fruit trees and nut trees and converted the bluestone-covered front yard into a veggie patch. Finally, I was living the dream.

It was at this point that a relative contacted my partner to say that there were plans for an Australian series of River Cottage and that I should definitely apply to become the host. I was already a massive fan of the UK series, as it was the only thing on TV that struck a chord with my own aspirations. I ummed and ahhed about applying, fully aware that if, *if* I were to succeed, my whole life would be turned upside down for better or for worse. Then I realised that I was being a little presumptuous and that there would be tens of thousands of people applying and that most of them would be more qualified, capable and camera-ready than me. So on the final day of applications, I sat down and feverishly typed out mine, hitting the send button at around 11:45pm. It was done. Come what may, my hat was now officially in the ring.

The next two months were a blur of phone calls, trips to Sydney and long nights staring at the ceiling above my bed until it finally came to a head one Friday afternoon in February. My phone rang, it was the production company, yes, yes, uh huh, right, ok then, see you in three weeks. I had twenty-one days to relocate to Central Tilba, a place on the New South Wales south coast that I'd never heard of, where I would be meeting the one and only Hugh Fearnley-Whittingstall and commencing work on River Cottage Australia.

When I arrived at the farm it was an 8-hectare blank canvas. Just an old house with a yard, a disused dairy, a couple of old silos and a boundary fence. It hadn't been farmed for over two decades and everything was in a slow spiral into disrepair. However, what the farm did have in spades was fertile soil and potential. Hugh was there for the first week to lend a hand and his expertise. We dug new garden beds outside the kitchen and we introduced a couple of laying hens to the old chook house. They were small but important steps.

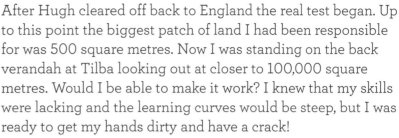

After Hugh cleared off back to England the real test began. Up to this point the biggest patch of land I had been responsible for was 500 square metres. Now I was standing on the back verandah at Tilba looking out at closer to 100,000 square metres. Would I be able to make it work? I knew that my skills were lacking and the learning curves would be steep, but I was ready to get my hands dirty and have a crack!

I've now been on the farm for nearly two years and when I look back and think about all the things that have happened, it makes my mind spin. There have been countless setbacks on every front. In the garden, seedlings have been decimated by wind, hail, birds and hungry insects. My first big crop of tomatoes was supposed to yield a tonne but, because of a haphazard watering schedule and a magnesium deficiency, only yielded a wheelbarrow full. Predators have attacked my chickens and ducks on numerous occasions. One night a fox forced its way through the mesh of my mobile chicken coop and killed all twenty-five birds inside in a single sitting. My goats escaped one night during a windstorm that blew over their electric fence, and they headed straight for the hills behind the farm. I searched for a full day to no avail then, on the second day, while standing on a high ridge, I heard a distant bleat from the dense scrub. I eventually found the whole herd, but finding them was one thing – getting them back to the farm was another matter entirely. One half decided they wanted to come home, the other half decided that they liked their new digs better and ran off deeper into the bush. It took me two whole days of running up and down steep hillsides, patiently cajoling, but with the occasional outburst of expletives, to get all eight back to the farm. These are just a few of the more major dramas that unfolded over the last couple of years but every day had its own unique challenges.

Don't get me wrong – for everything that went wrong there was something that made the drama melt away into a state of pure ecstasy. Things like tasting my first home-reared pork; drinking milk still warm from the udder; cracking open chook eggs to find yolks so vibrant that they look like they could be radioactive; and sharing a meal made with produce that I've grown with my beautiful partner, as my dog Digger goes doe-eyed and begs for scraps. Working outside under the influence of the seasons and all the individual beauty that they embody. The list goes on and on, but the thing that really left me awestruck was the vibrancy and hospitality of my small rural community. Neighbours quickly became friends, and a helping

hand, some sage advice or a friendly ear were always just a phone call away. For the first time in a long time the food that I was cooking wasn't disappearing over the pass to a stranger in a restaurant, it was being shared with people who shared my passion for honest, home-grown food.

There's no going back now – I'm totally hooked. The more time I spend working and learning on the farm, the more that I realise how much there is to learn. Every season builds upon the lessons and experiences of the last. It's given me an incredible appreciation of how much work it takes to produce quality food and a new-found respect for every ingredient that comes into my kitchen. An enormous amount of effort goes into raising vegetables and tending to livestock. It's easy to forget this when you have no connection or care as to how your food is produced. This lack of connection takes the joy out of food for me; it becomes a commodity rather than an essential part of my life that nourishes both body and spirit. Is all the effort worth it for a few ingredients that I could easily pick up for a song at the local supermarket? Without a shadow of a doubt.

I understand that not everyone has the opportunity to move out to the country and start farming for themselves. That doesn't mean that you can't play a meaningful role in how your food is produced. As consumers, we have a huge amount of influence. The first and most important thing that you can do is care. Care about how your food is being produced, care about who is reaping the benefits from its sale, care about how far it has to travel, and care about how it will benefit you. Next, start questioning the people who sell you your food. Where was it grown, is it organic, is it pasture- or grain-fed, is it at its best now or has it been in cold storage? Don't be shy about asking these things either. If your butcher, greengrocer, supermarket attendant or baker are passionate about the things they're selling then they'll be delighted that you're showing interest and be more than happy to answer. If they can't answer your questions then take your business to someone who can. Seek out farmers' markets and small retailers who take pride in what they're selling. It may be a touch more expensive but the food will be more nutrient-dense and there will be none of the hidden social and environmental costs that accompany the industrial food complex. If you eat less meat of a higher quality, favouring cheaper cuts or whole birds, along with seasonal, locally grown vegetables, then the price difference compared to what you can get in a supermarket will be negligible. The difference in flavour and nutrition, however, will be astronomical.

In addition to caring about the provenance of our food, the other important message that I hope you take from this book is that food should be a daily celebration. It should be something that brings together family and friends in good health and good times. Going to the effort of preparing a meal yourself and then sharing it with those you care about is one of life's simple pleasures. I've selected the recipes in this book to be simple, accessible and to celebrate the unique flavour of each ingredient. Don't be intimidated by ingredient lists and methods, just roll up your sleeves, invite some friends over and get cooking – you'll be glad that you did.

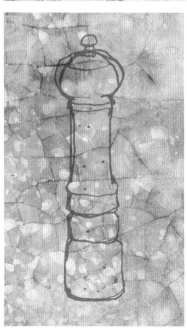

SEASONING

When seasoning dishes with salt flakes, I prefer to use Murray River pink salt – it's delicious and helps reduce salinity in one of Australia's most significant rivers. When seasoning with pepper, I like to use whole black peppercorns, freshly cracked in a mill.

BUTTER AND OIL

I use good quality unsalted butter in all my cooking, adding salt as required when seasoning the dish.

For general shallow frying and deep-frying I use a neutral-flavoured oil with a high smoke-point, such as rice bran, sunflower or canola, unless otherwise specified. When I want the flavour of the oil to be experienced in the dish, such as in a salad dressing or on some roasted veggies, I like to use an Australian extra-virgin olive oil.

If you're deep-frying without a digital probe thermometer, the temperature of the oil can be tested using a cube of bread or drop of batter. For a temperature of 170°C, toss the bread into the hot oil – if it turns golden brown in 20–25 seconds, then the oil is at the right temperature. For a temperature of 180°C, a small amount of batter will bubble up straight away.

Oil used for deep-frying can be reused: allow it to cool to room temperature, and pour it through a fine strainer into a glass jar. Reuse the oil until its colour has darkened considerably.

HOW TO STERILISE JARS

Sterilising jars before use prevents contamination and increases the longevity of homemade sauces and preserves. First, heat your oven to 120°C. Wash the jars and their metal lids in warm soapy water, then rinse them well and shake off excess water. Transfer the jars and lids to a baking tray, and place them in the oven for 15 minutes. Another option is to put the jars in the dishwasher and run a minimum wash on a high-temperature setting. Bottle hot sauces and preserves in hot jars, and cooled sauces and preserves in cold jars.

VEGETABLES & SALADS

Cooking without fruit, vegetables and herbs is like seeing the world in black and white. The edible plants that we lovingly sow, nurture and harvest bring a rainbow spectrum of colour and texture to the kitchen. They offer us cooks an almost infinite combination of flavours and their nourishing vitamins and minerals are essential to our health and wellbeing. In Australia we are particularly blessed with a wide range of micro-climates and growing zones, enabling our farmers and gardeners to grow nearly every edible plant imaginable, from apples to zucchini.

There was a time not that long ago in our food culture where vegetables were lacking a real presence in the kitchen. They were an afterthought to the meaty star of a meal and except for the universally appealing spud, were generally boiled to the very limit of palatability. As adults, how many of us have turned our nose up at certain vegetables because of the childhood memory of being forced to eat flaccid, flavourless greens. Fortunately, home cooks are beginning to acknowledge the myriad benefits that fruit, vegetables and herbs have to offer. Veggies are finally stepping out from the shadows and proudly asserting their place on our tables.

It's been inspirational to see Australians also starting to ask questions about the provenance and seasonality of their fruit and veg. We're starting to let the seasons act as our guide to get the most in terms of flavour, nutrition and economy. I love nothing more than heading out into the garden or down to the local farmers' market to see what's ripe for the picking. This is the inspiration for what I cook: a few tasty seasonal items in simple dishes, so that the unique flavours can be truly enjoyed.

We need to forget the notion that every variety of fruit and vegetable should be available year round. How boring – a world without seasons and none of the celebration and appreciation that comes from letting the natural cycle of the seasons dictate what is available. We'd miss the excitement of that first juicy peach, the first ripe tomato or the first crunchy, sweet peas of the season. What would you prefer – buying oranges picked yesterday by your local market gardener for part of the year, or having year-round access to oranges that were picked months ago on a distant continent? Personally, I would prefer to have amazing oranges for a short time than bland oranges year round.

If you've got the time and space, then the most satisfying way to have a supply of delicious fruit and vegetables is to grow them yourself. Whether you have acres of fertile soil or

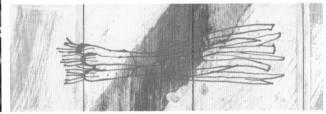

just a couple of pots on a sunny windowsill, with a little water, sun and love you can produce your own home-grown goodness. Just remember that plants really, really want to grow – it's up to us to make sure that they have everything they need to do so. There will always be a few setbacks: plants will die because you didn't water them enough, bugs will eat your seedlings in the dead of the night and birds will help themselves to that perfectly ripe piece of fruit that you were just about to harvest. Don't beat yourself up about your mistakes – growing your own fruit and veg should be an exciting and rewarding experience. Watch your garden and learn from it. If there's something not right it'll usually let you know way before it's too late. Observe as seeds sprout, new leaves unfold, flower buds develop and then burst like leafy fireworks. Watch as fruit slowly starts to form, grow and then ripen.

This is what growing your own food is about – an intimate dance with nature where you play a key part in getting to the grand finale. All those bumps on your gardening road are quickly forgotten the moment a tomato still warm from the sun explodes in your mouth. People have always waxed lyrical about the joy of eating freshly picked fruit and vegetables and it's not just self-indulgent cook/gardener prose – it's the stone cold truth. Something that you've grown yourself really does taste better. There's another layer to the flavour, one that can't be expressed using traditional taste descriptors. Home-grown produce fires up the satisfaction gland (trust me, it exists) in a way that nothing else can.

If you've never planted a seed or grown a plant in your life then don't despair – it's easy to get started. First you'll need some rich soil. Healthy plants grow out of healthy soil. If you're planting in the ground then scatter a few shovel loads of ripe compost over your garden beds and use a garden fork to gently incorporate it into the soil. If you're planting into pots then either find somewhere with a bit of fertile soil (the floodplains around rivers is a good place to start) and grab a couple of bucket loads or head to a gardening centre and buy the best organic potting mix you can afford. Next, you'll need some quality plants or seeds and I think that this is where most people go wrong. Steer clear of buying punnets of seedlings or plants from the local hardware mega store. They may be cheap but chances are they're also root-bound and undernourished. Instead, seek out a grower who raises quality heirloom varieties. They can usually be found at farmers' markets and the plants

that they sell will be robust, healthy and much more likely to survive through to harvest. Now that you've got the two key ingredients for a successful garden, with a little sunshine and regular watering you're well and truly on your way to your first delicious harvest.

If the idea of growing your own food still seems a little daunting, or you just don't have the space, then I highly recommend that you seek out a local community garden and get involved. It's how I learnt to grow veggies! Whether or not you get your own little patch will depend on the individual garden but one thing's for certain, you will learn heaps about the ancient craft of growing food. Gardeners generally will be happy to share with you the little tips and tricks that they have accumulated over their own gardening lives. It's a great way to get out and meet a diverse group of people who are united by a singular, worthy cause: growing food and eating it.

Growing your own food does take time and I know that spare time is somewhat of a luxury for many people. Just because you don't have time to grow it yourself doesn't mean that you can't enjoy freshly harvested produce that has been grown with wisdom and care. There has been an explosion of farmers' markets around this country in the last decade. From the concrete capitals to two-horse towns, farmers are setting up their trestle tables and selling their produce. The thing that I really love about farmers' markets is that you get to look the person who grew your food in the eye, you get to talk to them, joke with them and ask questions. There is nowhere to hide excuses: they grew it, harvested it and now they're handing it over to you. No middlemen, no warehouses and no interstate transportation. As consumers it's up to us to support these hard-working farmers. Thanks to them we can enjoy the spoils of nutritious, lovingly grown produce when the pressure of our own lives prevents us from growing it ourselves.

I hope that after reading this you are as excited about your fruit and veg as I am. There is so much to be inspired by and so many flavours to explore. All of these recipes aim to celebrate the best that fresh fruit and veg have to offer and are inspired by the ever-changing bounty of the seasons. So get your hands dirty with some delicious garden produce and add a little colour to your kitchen palette.

Watermelon is the perfect antidote to working in the garden on a hot summer's day. Cut into slices and enjoyed in the shade, it can rejuvenate even the most wilted, sun-drenched worker. However, this rosy melon shouldn't be limited to being eaten *au naturel*. Why not give it a crack in a salad and elevate it from a snack to a meal?

Watermelon Salad

SERVES 4

½ watermelon, peeled, cut into bite-sized chunks, seeds removed

Salt flakes

½ red onion, finely sliced

1 Lebanese cucumber, deseeded, cut in half lengthways and sliced

Small handful each of red and yellow cherry tomatoes, halved

Handful of basil leaves, roughly torn

1 teaspoon apple cider vinegar

Juice of ½ lime

Extra-virgin olive oil

Pepper

Put the watermelon in a serving bowl and sprinkle over a little salt. Add the onion, cucumber, cherry tomatoes and basil leaves to the watermelon.

Dress the salad with the vinegar, the lime juice, a splash of olive oil and a couple of generous twists of pepper. Serve as a refreshingly light lunch or as a side dish for a summer barbecue.

Pears work beautifully alongside savoury, salty ingredients such as blue cheese. Here, Hugh has used air-dried ham as an alternative partner. This salad makes a great starter – or pile it onto garlic-rubbed bruschetta for lunch.

Hugh's Pear, Ham and Rosemary Salad with Pecans

SERVES 4

2 ripe, medium-sized pears

2 tablespoons extra-virgin olive oil

1 teaspoon chopped rosemary

Pinch of dried chilli flakes (optional)

Lemon juice

Salt and pepper

3–4 handfuls of rocket

About 30g very thinly sliced air-dried ham, such as prosciutto

50g (½ cup) pecans (or walnuts), roughly chopped

Peel and quarter the pears, remove their cores then slice each quarter into two or three pieces. Put the pear pieces in a bowl, add the olive oil, rosemary, chilli flakes (if using), a little squeeze of lemon juice and a twist of salt and pepper. Gently combine.

Arrange the rocket on serving plates, or on one large platter. Place the pear pieces on top, reserving the juices in the bowl. Pull the ham into shreds and lay these over the pears, then scatter over the pecans or walnuts. Finish with a trickle of the oily, rosemary-spiked pear juices, and serve.

You can't miss a persimmon tree in a winter orchard: after all the leaves and fruit of the other trees have fallen, persimmons hang on the bare branches, proud and bright, like forgotten summer jewels. There are two main varieties – the non-astringent Fuyu and the astringent Hachiya – and it is important to understand the difference. A Fuyu can be eaten while still a little under-ripe, when it will have a pleasant crunch like an apple and a mild, lightly sweet, slightly tart flavour. The Hachiya, however, must be bordering on over-ripe to be palatable. If you eat one before it's time the flavour will be bitter and leave you with a fuzzy-mouth feel. If you wait until it's ripe, the fruit will be meltingly soft and sweet, with a hint of spice.

Persimmon lends itself not only to the sweet realm of desserts and baking but is also quite comfortable alongside roasted joints of white meat or as the star of a spritely salad, like this one.

Persimmon Salad

SERVES 2

2 ripe Fuyu persimmons, sliced into thin discs

Handful of rocket leaves

Small handful of hazelnuts, roasted, skinned, roughly chopped

1 ball fior di latte, torn into bite-sized chunks

DRESSING

1 teaspoon honey

½ teaspoon Dijon mustard

20ml white wine vinegar

60ml (¼ cup) extra-virgin olive oil

Salt and pepper

Pop the persimmon discs into a salad bowl with the rocket. Add the roasted hazelnuts and torn fior di latte to the bowl.

To make the dressing, combine all the ingredients, along with a little salt and pepper in a small bowl and quickly whisk with a fork. Pour the dressing over the salad and give the whole thing a good toss. Enjoy immediately!

As anyone who has grown zucchini can attest, by the end of summer you practically have them coming out of your ears. Not that I'm complaining — there are a thousand and one delicious recipes that call on this humble veggie, though few are as simple as this raw zucchini salad. For the best results, seek out the small, tender ones. If you're growing your own this is an excellent way to use the young fruit before they turn into hulking, woody giants.

Raw Zucchini Salad

SERVES 4

2 garlic cloves, finely chopped

1 teaspoon Dijon mustard

Juice of 1 lemon

Extra-virgin olive oil

4 small, tender zucchini; a mixture of yellow and green would be ideal

Small bunch of flat-leaf parsley, leaves roughly torn

Small bunch of mint, leaves roughly torn

Mix the garlic with the Dijon, lemon juice and a good glug of the olive oil.

Grab a sharp vegetable peeler and slice the zucchini into thin ribbons, skin and all. Put the zucchini in a salad bowl along with the mint and parsley leaves. Pour the dressing over and give it a good toss to ensure an even coating.

Serve immediately alongside some barbecued meats or on a flavour-packed veggie burger.

Keep an eye out for these fiery little fellas at farmers' markets, or try growing some at home. Black radishes have a bigger, more peppery kick than the average radish, so I like to cut them very finely and chill them out a little with a dollop of mayo. I tend to use them as a powerful condiment to serve with whole roasted fish like bream or flathead.

Black Radish Remoulade

SERVES **4** AS A SIDE DISH

4 black radishes, cleaned and cut into fine matchsticks (or 2 bunches of red radishes, finely sliced)

Small bunch of chives, finely chopped

Small bunch of flat-leaf parsley, finely chopped

MAYONNAISE

1 free-range egg yolk

Pinch of salt

1 teaspoon white wine vinegar

½ teaspoon Dijon mustard

100ml mild-flavoured oil (rice bran or grapeseed are perfect)

Pour some boiling water over the radishes to soften them. Drain straight away and pat them dry with paper towel.

To make the mayonnaise, combine the yolk, salt, vinegar and mustard in a mixing bowl. Whisk the ingredients together and slowly pour in the oil until the mixture has emulsified.

Combine the chopped chives and parsley with the radishes and the mayonnaise. Stir well and serve straight away.

No table at a barbecue would be complete without
a bowl of coleslaw. Everyone has their own version
and everyone happens to make the best in the known
universe. I like to use a wombok cabbage for mine.
I like the finer leaves, and find that the simpler the
ingredient list the better the slaw. No bells or whistles
here, just good fresh ingredients and some homemade
mayo. Of course, if you don't have time to whip up your
own mayo then some store-bought stuff will work fine.

Wombok Slaw

SERVES 4

**1 small wombok, divided into
leaves, fibrous stems cut away**

**3 spring onions, trimmed and
thinly sliced on an angle**

**4 red radishes, trimmed and
cut into matchsticks**

**Small bunch of flat-leaf parsley,
finely chopped**

**Small bunch of chives,
finely chopped**

**100ml mayonnaise
(see page 38)**

Salt and pepper

Stack the wombok leaves on top of each other and use a sharp
knife to thinly shred them. Pile the shredded leaves into
a large salad bowl. Add the spring onions, radishes, parsley
and chives to the salad bowl.

Spoon over the mayonnaise, season with a little salt and
pepper and then give the whole lot a good mix to make sure
everything is evenly covered and serve.

If you don't have enough time for a veggie patch you can still harvest your own fresh greens. They can be found pretty much anywhere there are people, they're highly nutritious and, most importantly, they're free. I'm talking about weeds. Once you get your eye in and learn what varieties you can and can't eat, you quickly realise that edible weeds are everywhere. I can't walk down the street in town or around the farm without spotting a potential free feed. In this recipe the leaves are dressed with a nettle pesto. There is no need for vinegar because the low levels of oxalic acid present in many of the weeds provide the sharpness.

Weed Pickers' Salad with Nettle Pesto Dressing

CHOOSE ENOUGH OF THE FOLLOWING VARIETIES TO MAKE A SALAD FOR 4:

Fat hen

Wood sorrel

Nasturtium leaves and flowers

Plantain

Wild fennel fronds

Purslane

Chickweed

Cobblers pegs

Warrigal greens

NETTLE PESTO

2 big, gloved handfuls of nettle leaves

2 garlic cloves, peeled

80g (½ cup) macadamias

2 tablespoons grated Parmesan

200ml extra-virgin olive oil, plus some extra to dress the salad

Salt and pepper

First make the pesto. Bring a pot of salty water to the boil and pop in the nettle leaves. Cook for about 1 minute, then drain the leaves and transfer them to a bowl of iced water. When the leaves have cooled, drain them again, wrap them in a tea towel and give them a good squeeze to get out any excess moisture.

Pop the leaves into the bowl of a food processor and add the garlic, macadamias and Parmesan, then give it a good whiz while you steadily pour in the olive oil. Give the pesto a quick taste, adjust the seasonings to your liking, then transfer it to a container and pour over a little more oil.

Combine the wild leaves in a mixing bowl. Take 3 tablespoons of the pesto and add some extra oil so that it is light enough to dress the salad. Pour the pesto dressing over the salad and give it a good toss. Serve straight away. Keep any leftover pesto in the fridge to use later. You could fold it through gnocchi or have it on toast with some grilled cheese.

Warrigal greens were one of the first native plants consumed by early European settlers. They were picked and cooked by the crew of the *Endeavour* to help fight scurvy, though you don't need to be a vitamin C–deficient sailor to enjoy this leafy vegetable. Serving them with this buttery, garlic sauce is a great way to incorporate a bit of bush tucker into your next roast dinner.

Warrigal Greens with Garlic and Butter

SERVES 4 AS A SIDE DISH

Oil, for frying

3 garlic cloves, peeled and sliced

3 good handfuls of Warrigal greens, woody stems trimmed

Knob of butter

Juice of ½ a lemon

Place a pan over a medium–high heat, add a splash of cooking oil and then fry the garlic. As soon as the garlic starts to colour, add the Warrigal greens and move them around vigorously while they wilt. After a minute, remove the greens from the heat and pop them in a colander or on a clean tea towel to drain off any excess water.

Return the pan to the heat and add the knob of butter. As soon as it starts to foam, return the greens to the pan, add the lemon juice and give everything a good stir to evenly coat.

Serve straight away with a juicy chunk of grilled or roasted meat.

When Hugh visited the farm, I learnt that he is a great lover of nettles. In the early spring, he gathers the tender, growing tops by the (carefully protected) handful and uses them in soups, risottos and simple recipes like this one. It requires only a small amount and is a great one to try if you're new to nettles.

Hugh's Nettle Bubble and Squeak

SERVES 2

Around 50g or half a colander of nettle tops

2–3 tablespoons rapeseed or sunflower oil

4–6 spring onions, trimmed and chopped

About 300g cooked potato, roughly chopped, or leftover mash

Salt and pepper

Poached or fried free-range egg, to serve

Pick over the nettle tops and wash thoroughly. Discard the tougher stalks. Bring a large pan of well-salted water to the boil and throw in the nettles. Bring back to the boil, cook for just 2 minutes, then drain in a colander. When the nettles are cool enough to handle, squeeze them to extract as much water as possible, then chop them. This, incidentally, is a good basic technique for preparing (and de-stinging!) nettles for all kinds of recipes.

Heat 2 tablespoons of oil in a medium, non-stick frying pan over a medium heat. Add the spring onions and sauté for a couple of minutes. Add the chopped potato/mash and cook for up to 10 minutes, stirring often, until it starts to colour. You may want to add a little more oil at this stage and you'll probably need to use the edge of a spatula to scrape up some of the lovely crusty bits from the bottom of the pan.

Add the chopped nettles, then fry for 2–3 more minutes, stirring them into the potatoes. The finished texture will vary: if you use mash, you can squash your bubble and squeak into a rough cake, fried golden brown on both sides. If you use chopped cooked spuds, just keep tossing or flipping different parts of it – you'll end up with a looser, hash-like consistency. In both cases keep cooking till you have plenty of crispy golden bits.

Season generously with salt and pepper and serve your bubble and squeak with a poached or fried egg. This is also great served with any leftovers from a roast chicken, or pork, or some good sausages.

You really just have to love a well-roasted potato,
with a golden, crispy skin and a delicate fluffy interior.
Whether served with a slab of perfectly roasted meat
or simply tossed into a bowl and enjoyed by themselves,
there's always room for roasted spuds in my life.
Feel free to peel the skins, though I like to leave them
on because they crisp up beautifully when roasted.
If you're a little short on duck fat, you can substitute
with some oil.

Duck Fat Roast Potatoes

SERVES **4** AS A SIDE DISH

500g floury potatoes, such as Coliban or King Edward

2 tablespoons duck fat

Small bunch of rosemary, leaves picked

Salt flakes

Cut the potatoes into big, bite-sized pieces, skins and all. Pop all the spuds into a pot of cold, well-salted water, bring to a simmer and cook for about 10 minutes.

Preheat the oven to 200°C and place a deep-sided roasting tray in the oven.

Once the potatoes are cooked enough that the tip of a knife can be gently pushed in, still with a little resistance, strain them. Toss them in the colander vigorously so that the surface is roughed up, or use a little pressure from a fork. The roughed-up surface lets more heat and fat penetrate the potato while it's roasting, which means more crispy bits, which means more smiles all round.

Remove the hot tray from the oven and add the duck fat – it will melt straight away. Toss in the potatoes and rosemary and sloosh them around with a spoon to ensure that every potato is well coated.

Put the tray in the oven and roast for around 30 minutes or until the spuds are golden and crispy. Drain the potatoes on paper towel to remove any excess fat and season liberally with salt.

One of the best things about having my own veggie garden is the year-round bounty of crisp, fresh greens that it supplies. It's always there to whip together a quick salad, add some colour to dinner, or in this case, freshen up some good ol' eggs for breakfast. The freshness of the garden greens is beautifully balanced by the cream and the rich, runny yolks.

Baked Eggs with Garden Greens and Cream

SERVES 4

2 kale leaves, stems trimmed

1 silverbeet leaf, stem trimmed

Small handful of English spinach, torn

Small handful of sorrel, torn

8 free-range eggs

250ml (1 cup) double cream

Small chunk of Parmesan

Salt and pepper

Preheat your oven to 180°C.

Bring a pot of lightly salted water to the boil. Dunk the kale and silverbeet leaves in the boiling water for about 30 seconds. Once the leaves have softened, remove them from the water and roughly chop them with a knife.

Divide the kale, silverbeet, spinach and sorrel leaves evenly among four ovenproof bowls or ramekins, leaving a little well in the centre of each. Crack two eggs into each well, pour some cream over the greens and shave a little Parmesan over the whole lot. Season generously with salt and pepper and then pop all four bowls in the oven. Bake for around 15 minutes. The egg whites should be set and the yolks still runny. Remove from the oven.

Serve with slices of toasted sourdough loaf (see pages 218–19) that's been slathered with cultured butter (see page 240).

This is, by far, my favourite way to eat broccoli. Separating the florets from the stalks means that nothing goes to waste and that you can control how long each part is cooked for. Teamed with aromatic herbs, fluffy couscous and a hit of tangy lemon, this should sway even the most vocal broccoli bashers.

Broccoli and Walnut Couscous

SERVES 4

370g (2 cups) couscous

Oil, for frying

1 red onion, finely sliced

1 celery stick, finely sliced

1 head of broccoli, stalk finely sliced, florets shaved

2 garlic cloves, sliced

Juice and zest of 1 lemon

Salt and pepper

Small bunch each of flat-leaf parsley, mint and chives, roughly chopped

Handful of walnuts, toasted and roughly chopped

Extra-virgin olive oil

Bring 500ml of water to the boil and then pour it over the couscous, cover and let stand for 5 minutes. Remove the cover and fluff the couscous with a fork, then set it aside some place warm.

Heat a frypan over a medium heat, add a little oil and sauté the onion, celery and broccoli stalks for a few minutes, until everything has softened. Add the garlic and broccoli florets and continue frying until the florets are starting to colour and the garlic is soft and aromatic. Remove the pan from the heat, pour over the juice from the lemon and season with salt and pepper. Fork the fried vegetables through the couscous along with the herbs, walnuts, lemon zest and a splash of olive oil.

Enjoy as a salad by itself or as a herby side to a spicy tagine.

The flavour of a freshly dug carrot has to be tasted to be believed. I like to give them a good clean and quickly roast them (skins and all) and then serve them with earthy hazelnuts, a handful of sweet currants and some tangy, creamy labne. If you can't get your hands on any labne, or don't have time to make it, you can always use a couple of spoonfuls of thick, natural yoghurt.

Roasted Baby Carrot Salad with Labne and Hazelnuts

SERVES 4 AS A SIDE DISH

2 bunches baby carrots, cleaned, stalks trimmed to 5mm

Olive oil, for roasting

Salt and pepper

70g (½ cup) hazelnuts, roasted, skins removed, roughly chopped

35g (¼ cup) currants

Small bunch of coriander, leaves picked

125ml (½ cup) labne (see page 246)

Extra-virgin olive oil

Preheat your oven to 200°C.

Toss the carrots in a bowl with a splash of olive oil and a pinch each of salt and pepper. Give the bowl a good shake to ensure that the carrots are evenly coated and then transfer to a baking tray. Roast for about 30 minutes until browned and softened.

Remove the carrots from the oven and allow to cool slightly. Transfer to a mixing bowl and add the hazelnuts and currants, giving it all a good shake to combine. Transfer to a serving platter and scatter over coriander leaves, labne and a light drizzle of extra-virgin olive oil.

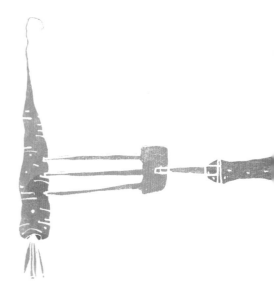

Green Beans with Labne, Shallots and Almonds

SERVES 4 AS A SIDE DISH

500g green beans, topped and tailed

2 shallots, thinly sliced

Extra-virgin olive oil

Salt flakes

125ml (½ cup) labne (see page 246)

Handful of slivered almonds

Put a big pot of salty water on the stove and bring it to a vigorous boil. Toss the beans in the boiling water to cook for 2 minutes – they should still have the slightest crunch, there's nothing worse than flaccid beans. Drain the beans and toss them in a bowl with the thinly sliced shallots, a splash of olive oil and a generous sprinkle of salt flakes.

Transfer to a serving dish, then spoon over the labne and sprinkle over the slivered almonds. Serve immediately as a fresh side to a golden roast chicken (see page 144).

This hearty, brothy soup is a perfect warmer for a cool autumn lunch. The beans pack enough punch to make this a proper meal and the fresh veggies and smoky trout balance each other nicely, though the beating heart of this soup is the stock. If you don't have any, take a little time and make some – this is one recipe where the store-bought stuff just won't do!

Borlotti Broth with Garden Veggies and Smoked Trout

SERVES 4

1½ litres (6 cups) chicken stock (see page 208) or veggie stock (see page 59)

200g (1 cup) borlotti beans, soaked the night before and then drained

1 small bulb of fennel, very finely sliced

1 small head of radicchio, end trimmed, leaves roughly torn

½ small red onion, very finely sliced

1 garlic clove, finely sliced

1 x 400g smoked trout (see pages 110–11), skin and bones discarded

150g (1½ cups) Parmesan, shaved

Pepper

Pour the stock into a pot and bring to a simmer. Add the borlotti beans and simmer for 15 minutes or until the beans are tender.

As soon as the beans are cooked add the fennel, radicchio, onion and garlic and simmer for another couple of minutes. Flake the trout flesh a little. Ladle the soup into four bowls and scatter the smoked trout over the top along with a little shaved Parmesan and some pepper.

Serve while steaming hot, along with a slice of toasted, crusty bread.

There's nothing better on a cold winter's day than a big, steaming bowl of hearty soup. With veggies fresh from the winter garden, chewy roasted barley for a bit of body and a herby, spicy pesto for an extra kick of flavour, this soup will have you wishing that winter would never end.

Winter Vegetable Soup

SERVES **6**

220g (1 cup) pearl barley

Oil, for frying

2 leeks or 8 spring onions, thinly sliced

500g broccoli, stalks sliced, cut into florets

400g white cabbage, finely shredded

2 litres (8 cups) chicken stock (see page 208) or veggie stock (see page 59)

400g (2½ cups) podded green peas

PESTO

Large bunch of flat-leaf parsley, leaves picked

4 mild red chillies, seeded and chopped (optional)

4 cloves garlic, chopped

100g (1 cup) walnut halves

100g (1 cup) grated Parmesan

330ml (1⅓ cup) extra-virgin olive oil

Roast the barley in a large frypan over a medium heat until it smells nutty and has turned a deep brown in colour. This should take around 10 minutes, though keep an eye on it as it can quickly burn.

Transfer the roasted barley into a large saucepan of lightly salted water and bring to the boil. Reduce the heat to a simmer and cook uncovered for around half an hour or until the barley is soft and chewy. Drain the barley into a colander and pop to one side.

While the barley is cooking, heat a little oil in the frypan over a medium heat. Add the leeks or onions and cook for 10 minutes or until they are soft and golden. Add the broccoli stalks and cabbage and cook for 5 minutes or until they start to soften.

Pour in the stock and simmer for 20 minutes or until the broccoli stalks are tender. Add the broccoli florets, peas and barley and cook for 5 minutes or until the florets are tender.

To make the pesto, put the parsley, chillies (if using), garlic, walnuts and Parmesan in a food processor and process until roughly chopped. With the motor running slowly, add the oil until the pesto is thick.

Serve the vegetable soup topped with a generous dollop of pesto.

Stocks are the backbone of so many dishes in the kitchen that I can't recommend highly enough that you learn how to make a good one. It's really not hard and a vegetable stock is one of the quickest and easiest. This light veggie stock is the perfect foundation for a steamy broth or a fresh spring risotto. If you'd like to add a little more complexity to the flavour, you can roast the veggies in a hot oven for half an hour before adding them to the stockpot.

Veggie Stock

MAKES ABOUT 2 LITRES

**2 brown onions,
roughly chopped**

2 carrots, roughly chopped

**2 celery sticks,
roughly chopped**

**½ bulb of fennel,
roughly chopped**

1 leek, roughly chopped

**1 head of garlic, cut in half
horizontally**

2 tomatoes, chopped

Handful of button mushrooms

2 bay leaves

Small bunch of thyme

**Small bunch of flat-leaf
parsley stalks**

½ teaspoon black peppercorns

375ml (½ bottle) white wine

Combine all the ingredients in a large pot. Pour in enough cold water to cover everything and then about half again. Bring the stock gently to the boil, then reduce the heat to a simmer and let it bubble away, uncovered, for half an hour. Turn the heat off and gently ladle the stock through a fine sieve. If you're not planning on using it within the next three days, freeze it in cup-sized portions – that way it'll keep for months.

Veggie gardeners have known for years that the delicate green shoots of the pea plant, which appear well before the pods themselves have formed, are a delicious treat. The same goes for broad bean tops, which have a lovely leguminous flavour. Hugh's tart, perfect for a relaxed spring lunch, makes the most of this gorgeous early harvest. If you're not able to pick shoots from your own veggie patch, many supermarkets now stock pea shoots alongside their bagged salads. You can also substitute baby spinach or flat-leaf parsley leaves for some of the broad bean tops, and a store-bought tart case for the homemade pastry.

Hugh's Broad Bean and Pea Top Tart

SERVES **6–8**

SHORTCRUST PASTRY

200g plain flour

Pinch of salt

100g cold butter, cut into small cubes

About 50ml cold full cream milk

FILLING

Large knob of butter

2 brown onions, finely sliced

250–300g broad bean tops, or a mixture of pea shoots and bean tops

Salt and pepper

100g mature Cheddar, coarsely grated

200ml full cream milk

200ml double cream

2 whole free-range eggs, plus 1 egg yolk

Salt and pepper

Start with the pastry. Put the flour, salt and butter in a food processor, and pulse until the mixture has the consistency of breadcrumbs. Then, with the motor running, pour in the milk in a thin stream. Watch carefully and stop adding milk as soon as the dough comes together. Tip out onto a lightly floured board, knead a couple of times to make a smooth ball of dough, then wrap in cling film and chill for half an hour.

Meanwhile, heat the butter in a frying pan over a medium heat and add the onions. Fry very gently until soft and golden brown – a good 10–15 minutes. Add the broad bean tops (or pea shoots and broad bean tops) and cook for a few minutes, stirring often, until wilted. Season with salt and pepper.

Preheat the oven to 180°C. Roll out the pastry thinly, and use it to line a 25cm, loose-bottomed tart tin. Leave the excess pastry hanging over the edge. Prick the base all over with a fork, line with baking paper and baking beans or uncooked rice, put the tin on a baking tray and bake for 15 minutes. Remove the paper and beans, and bake for about 10 minutes more until the pastry looks cooked and lightly coloured. Trim off the excess pastry with a small knife. Leave the oven at 180°C.

Arrange the bean top and onion mixture over the pastry case. Scatter on the grated cheese. In a jug, whisk together the milk, cream, eggs and yolk and season with salt and pepper. Pour this custard into the tart (you may have a little left over, but fill it as full as you can). Slide the tart carefully into the oven and bake for about 40 minutes, or until lightly set and golden brown. Serve warm or cold.

I like to cook a galette for a leisurely summer lunch. Weighting the puff pastry gives it a dense, buttery texture but it still has a delicate flakiness. It's the perfect base for some ripe, garden-fresh tomatoes and some sweet, roasted red onions.

Tomato Galette

SERVES **6**

4 red onions, skin on, halved from roots to stalk

Olive oil, for roasting

Salt and pepper

2 sheets of frozen puff pastry, thawed

A mixture of half a dozen or so ripe tomatoes, cut into different shapes

Small bunch of thyme, leaves picked

Extra-virgin olive oil

Preheat your oven to 200°C. Line a large, flat oven tray with baking paper.

Place the onions skin-side down on a baking tray. Splash a little olive oil over them, season liberally with salt and pepper, then slide the tray into the oven and bake for 25–30 minutes, or until tender.

Put the sheets of pastry on the lined oven tray so they snugly fit within its rectangular shape, trimming as needed. Lay another sheet of baking paper on top of the pastry and then place another oven tray the same size as the first one on top of that. Weigh both trays down with a couple of ovenproof pots and pop it in the oven along with the onions. Bake for around 20 minutes or until the pastry is golden and cooked all over.

Remove the cooked pastry and onions from the oven and take the top oven tray off the pastry.

Scoop out the soft onion flesh and scatter it evenly over the pastry, all the way to the edges. Lay the tomatoes on top of the onion. Sprinkle over the thyme leaves and season well with salt and pepper.

Turn the oven up to 220°C and place the galette back in the oven. Cook for around 10 minutes or until the tomatoes have softened and coloured a little around the edges. Remove from the oven, drizzle over a little extra-virgin olive oil, cut up into slices and serve straight away with a fresh green salad.

At the end of summer there is always a glut of super-ripe tomatoes. To preserve the most iconic of summer's spoils for the long and tomato-less winter, get some friends together, chip in and buy a passata mill, and spend a sunny afternoon making passata. Essentially just a tomato purée, passata is most welcome come winter for enlivening long, slow braises or for reducing with some onion, garlic and chilli for a simple pasta sauce.

Tomato Passata

MAKES JARLOADS

All the ripe tomatoes that you can get your hands on

Invite a couple of friends over, get a big trestle table out and set up a bit of a production line. The first role is the sorter, whose responsibility it is to ensure that no dud fruit goes through to the passata. This position will require someone with an unwavering eye for quality and quick hands. Next we have the top-chopper. Fearless with a sharp knife, the top-chopper cuts the finest sliver off the top of the tomato to remove the eye. Next we have the squeezer. As the name suggests, this person's role is to squeeze out excess liquid and seeds from the topped tomatoes. The best squeezers use a double-handed approach. Finally there is the loader and cranker, who has to fill the hopper of the passata mill while continually cranking the auger. The end result is a steady stream of vibrant red tomato purée and the all-permeating smell of the crushed fruit.

Switch the roles from time to time so no one gets bored. Or, if you only have a small amount of tomatoes, don't tell your friends and do everything yourself – that way you won't have to share the spoils.

Once all the fruit is puréed, use a funnel and ladle to fill your sterilised jars (see page 23). Pop the lids on firmly and then arrange the jars in a big pot that has a tea towel on the bottom and a couple wound between the jars so they don't touch. Fill the pot with enough water to submerge the jars. Bring the water to the boil and leave it at a steady boil for a couple of hours to sterilise and preserve the passata.

Let the jars cool, then dry them, stick on a label with the date and pop them in the larder or pantry. They'll keep well and truly until next year's passata-making day. Assuming you don't eat them all in the meantime!

I'm happy to come out and say that I'm not the biggest fan of raw capsicum, but cook it a little to bring out that sweet, peppery flavour and I'm there! When the garden is groaning under the weight of capsicums and tomatoes at the end of summer, I like to make a batch of peperonata every week to have in the fridge. It's great with pretty much any meat and can be used with a handful of spaghetti to make a frugal, fast but delicious dinner. I don't cook mine for as long as tradition requires – I prefer to have the veggies just softened for a lively, summery taste.

Peperonata

MAKES 1 LITRE

6 capsicums, preferably a mix of colours, halved, seeds and fibres removed

4 Roma tomatoes, cut top to bottom into quarters

Olive oil, for frying

1 brown onion, finely sliced

4 garlic cloves, finely sliced

Salt and pepper

1 lemon

Handful of basil leaves, roughly torn

Cut the capsicums into 2cm squares. Remove the seeds from the tomatoes and cut into strips about 5mm across.

Heat some oil in a pan over a medium heat, add the onion and sauté for a couple of minutes until it is just starting to colour. Add the capsicums and continue gently frying for around 5 minutes, or until they have started to soften. Add the garlic and fry for a further minute, then add the tomatoes and fry for another 2 or 3 minutes. Season liberally with salt and pepper, squeeze over the juice from the lemon and toss in the torn basil leaves.

To serve, toss the peperonata through a bowl of freshly cooked spaghetti or spread over a pizza base with some tomato paste.

If you're like me, sometimes you just need something deep-fried. Hot, fatty and crispy, veggie pakoras tick all the boxes for deep-fried satisfaction. The simple chickpea batter is a coat of armour that can be worn by almost any vegetable, making this a splendid recipe for using up those bits and bobs of left-over veg you have in the fridge.

Veggie Pakoras with Minty Yoghurt

SERVES 4

300g chickpea (besan) flour

1 teaspoon chilli powder

½ teaspoon turmeric powder

Water, as needed

1 litre (4 cups) rice bran oil (or similar), for deep-frying

½ head of cauliflower, cut into small, bite-sized pieces

1 potato, cut into 1cm thick slices

1 eggplant, cut into 1cm thick slices

Salt flakes

MINTY YOGHURT

250ml (1 cup) natural yoghurt (see page 245)

1 teaspoon caster sugar

Juice and zest of 1 lemon

Small bunch of mint, leaves picked

Combine the chickpea flour, chilli powder and turmeric powder in a mixing bowl. Slowly pour in about half a cup of water and use a whisk to bring the batter together. It should be pretty runny, though thick enough to coat the back of a spoon.

Fill a large, heavy-based saucepan with the oil and bring it up to around 180°C.

Combine the yoghurt, sugar, juice and zest of the lemon and the mint leaves in a bowl. Give it a quick whizz with a hand blender and pop it to one side. If you don't have a hand blender, finely chop the mint and mix it together by hand.

To check if the oil is hot enough, spoon a tiny amount of batter into the pot – if the batter bubbles up straight away you're good to go.

Dip the veggies in the batter and then deep-fry them, working in batches so that you don't overcrowd the pot. As soon as the batter is golden and crispy, use a slotted spoon to remove the pakoras from the oil and then let them drain on some paper towel.

Season the crispy pakoras with a sprinkling of salt and serve them hot with the minty yoghurt.

Spring is a beautiful time of year at the farm. The flowers and trees are blossoming, the birds are busy feeding their chicks and there is a hint of summer's heat in the air. It's also the season of the globe artichoke. I watch with great excitement as the plants start to throw up their immature flower heads. Artichokes can be a little intimidating as an ingredient, but don't let that stop you from enjoying them. Eating an artichoke can be as simple as peeling off the tough outer leaves and dunking the raw inner leaves in a flavour-packed dip such as this bagna cauda.

Fresh Artichokes with Bagna Cauda

SERVES 4

4 cloves garlic, peeled

300ml full cream milk

10 anchovy fillets in oil, drained

180ml (¾ cup) extra-virgin olive oil

1 tablespoon white wine vinegar

4 artichokes

To make the bagna cauda, place the garlic, milk and anchovies into a small pan and simmer over a medium heat for 10 minutes. Transfer the mixture to a food processor and combine until the mixture is smooth. While the motor is running, gradually add the olive oil and vinegar and process until creamy. Check the seasoning: the bagna cauda should be salty and tangy.

To prepare the artichokes, simply peel away the tough outer leaves. When the leaves start to turn white and soft at the base you can start to eat them. Only the lighter coloured parts of the leaves are edible, and as you work your way towards the centre of the artichoke you'll be able to eat more and more of the leaf.

Eggplants have a fantastic meatiness about them. The long and thin Japanese eggplants are perfect for popping under a grill or on a barbecue plate. As the skin blisters and chars over the coals, the smokiness delicately works its way into the creamy flesh. Freshen it up with some parsley and lemon juice, and this flavour-packed dip comes alive on the palate.

Chunky Eggplant Dip

SERVES 4

5–6 Japanese eggplants

Olive oil, for grilling and frying

1 medium brown onion, finely sliced

1 mild red chilli, deseeded and finely chopped

2 garlic cloves, finely sliced

½ teaspoon ground cumin

½ teaspoon smoked paprika

Juice of 1 lemon

Salt and pepper

½ bunch of flat-leaf parsley, roughly chopped

Quickly pierce each eggplant a couple of times with a fork, then cut in half lengthways. Lay the eggplants cut-side down on a baking tray, splash a little olive oil over them and slide them under a hot grill (or you can grill them on a barbecue). Grill for around 10 minutes or until the skin is charred and the flesh is tender. Remove them from the grill and when they're cool enough to handle, scoop the flesh away from the skin and into a colander, so that any excess juice can drain away.

Heat a frypan over a medium heat, add a little oil and sauté the onion for a couple of minutes until soft and translucent. Add the chilli, garlic, cumin and paprika and cook for another 5 minutes or so until everything is soft and aromatic. Add the eggplant to the pan and smash it up a little with a fork, then give everything a good toss to combine. Season with lemon juice, salt and pepper and finish off with a little chopped parsley.

Serve straight away with some barbecued red meat, or pop it in the fridge to cool and let the flavours develop, then spread it thickly on some toasted sourdough loaf (see pages 218–19).

The silken texture and smoky flavour of a grilled eggplant is a wonderful way to enrich a traditional gnocchi. I know that there are purists who would admonish me for including eggs in this recipe, let alone eggplant. As much as I respect tradition, sometimes a little experimentation can lead to delicious results. If you can't get your hands on white eggplants, you can always substitute one black eggplant.

Eggplant Gnocchi with Sage Burnt Butter

SERVES 4

4 floury potatoes, such as Coliban or King Edward, peeled

4 small white eggplants (or 1 large black eggplant), cut in half lengthways

Olive oil, for roasting

Salt and pepper

2 free-range eggs, lightly whisked

300g (2 cups) plain flour

50g (½ cup) Parmesan, finely grated, plus extra to serve

100g butter

Oil, for frying

3–4 Japanese eggplants, tops removed, cut into long strips

Small handful of sage leaves

Small bunch of flat-leaf parsley, roughly chopped

Steam the potatoes in a colander over a pot of simmering water, or in a steamer; cover and cook for about 20 minutes or until tender. When cooked, set them on the bench to steam off any excess moisture.

Preheat your oven to 180°C.

Use the tip of a knife to score a grid into the cut sides of the white eggplants, as deep as possible without piercing the skin. Place them skin-side down on an oven tray, drizzle over a little olive oil, season with salt and pepper and bake for 25 minutes or until they become very soft.

The spuds and the eggplants should be ready about the same time, which is perfect because they both have to be warm to make the gnocchi.

Mash the potatoes with a masher or put through a mouli and season with a little salt and pepper.

Scrape the flesh out of the cooked eggplants, break it apart with a fork and add it to the potato.

Pour the whisked eggs over the eggplant flesh and potato. Sprinkle over the flour and grated Parmesan and gently bring everything together to form a dough.

Sprinkle a little flour onto a clean bench and turn the dough out. Give it the slightest kneading to form a delicate, dry dough. Divide the dough into four balls, then roll each ball into a long cylinder with a diameter of around 2cm. Use a sharp knife to cut each cylinder into 3cm pieces.

Bring a large pot of salted water to the boil.

Heat a frypan over a medium–high heat, add half the butter and a little oil and then fry the slices of Japanese eggplant until they are soft and golden. Just before the eggplants are cooked, toss in the sage leaves and a little more butter. Continue cooking until the sage leaves have crisped and the butter is brown.

While the eggplants are cooking, drop about half the gnocchi into the boiling water. They cook quite quickly – they're ready when they start floating to the surface. Use a slotted spoon to remove the gnocchi from the water, shake off any excess water, then add the gnocchi to the frypan with the eggplant slices and sage. Repeat with the remaining gnocchi. Toss everything gently together and add the chopped parsley.

To serve, divide among four plates, sprinkle some Parmesan over the top and enjoy right away.

No one has the time to cook an elaborate dinner every night – sometimes a simple pasta dish is all you need. Some fresh greens from the garden, a kick of chilli and a couple of spoonfuls of fresh ricotta make for a flavour-packed weeknight dinner.

Spaghetti with Rainbow Chard, Chilli and Ricotta

SERVES 4

350g spaghetti

Small bunch of rainbow chard

Olive oil, for frying

1 brown onion, finely sliced

3 garlic cloves, finely sliced

1 mild red chilli, finely sliced

Extra-virgin olive oil

Salt and pepper

4 tablespoons ricotta (see page 244)

Bring a pot full of lightly salted water to the boil and cook the spaghetti to al dente.

Separate the leaves and stem of the chard, then finely slice them both.

Heat a frypan over a medium heat, add a little olive oil and sauté the onion and chard stems until soft, then add the garlic and chilli and continue frying for about 2 minutes. Add the thinly sliced chard leaves and cook for another 5 minutes or until the leaves are soft and wilted.

Add the cooked spaghetti to the pan along with a glug of extra-virgin olive oil and then season with salt and pepper. Divide the spaghetti among four bowls and crumble over the fresh ricotta. Sprinkle with some more pepper, if you like, and serve.

After the heat of summer, when the days start getting cooler and wetter, a trip to the nearest pine forest is always on my agenda. When forestry workers first imported pine tree seedlings they also imported a few hidden passengers that had long been living among the fallen needles – mushrooms. There is scant knowledge available about the edibility of Australia's native fungi, whereas the introduced Europeans come with centuries of tried and tested experience. The two varieties that will most likely make it into my basket are Saffron Milk Caps and Slippery Jacks. If you've never been mushrooming and you're unsure how to identify the edible varieties then it's best to go with someone in the know or be extremely careful to identify any mushrooms you pick before you cook them and feed them to your family.

Pappardelle with Wild Mushrooms

SERVES 4

PASTA

400g (3¼ cups) hard white bread flour

4 free-range eggs

Semolina, for dusting

MUSHROOM SAUCE

400g Slippery Jack mushrooms

400g Saffron Milk Cap mushrooms

Oil, for frying

3 garlic cloves, finely chopped

125ml (½ cup) white wine

250ml (1 cup) pure cream

Small bunch of wood sorrel leaves and flowers, rinsed and dried (or some finely chopped flat-leaf parsley if you can't find any sorrel)

To make the pasta, mound the flour onto a clean work bench and make a well in the centre. Crack the eggs into the well and then use a fork to break them apart so that the yolks and the whites are combined. Using your fingers, start to work the flour into the eggs until everything has come together to form a sticky yellow dough. Dust the bench with a little more flour and knead the dough until it is smooth and glossy (about 10 minutes).

Wrap the dough in some cling film and pop it in the fridge to rest for at least 30 minutes.

Once the dough is rested, lightly flour the bench, divide the dough into four chunks and roll each out to a thickness of around 3mm. To make the pappardelle, lightly dust each sheet with semolina then fold in half, then half again to make a sort of flat roll. Take a sharp knife and cut the rolled sheets at 3cm intervals, unfold and hey presto, long, thick strands of delicious pappardelle!

Lightly dust a tray with some semolina, unfold all of the pasta, and pop it on the tray until you're ready to cook it.

Place a large pot of salty water on the stove and bring it to the boil.

To prepare the Slippery Jacks, use a paring knife to peel the skin from the top of the mushrooms, discard the stalk and thinly slice the cap. To prepare the Saffron Milk Caps, give them a good rinse in cold water, pat dry, discard the stem and then thinly slice them.

Place a deep-sided frypan over a medium heat, add a splash of oil and fry the garlic until softened, then turn the heat up

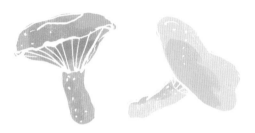

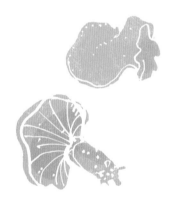

to high, add a little more oil and fry the mushrooms. Once the mushrooms have coloured and softened, reduce the heat to medium, add the white wine to the pan and reduce it to a third of its original volume.

Put the pasta into the boiling water to cook for 3 minutes or until al dente.

While the pasta is cooking, add the cream to the mushrooms and reduce for a minute or so, or until the cream is thick and bubbly. Drain the pasta and add it to the mushrooms and cream. Give it all a good toss to evenly coat the pasta, add half the wood sorrel leaves and season with salt and pepper.

Transfer the pasta to four bowls, garnish with the remaining wood sorrel and serve straight away.

Every year I like to add a couple of Golden Nugget
pumpkins to the rest of my spring plantings. They
don't grow on a wild vine like other pumpkins but on
a compact bush like a zucchini. Come high summer,
the little bushes are laden with orange orbs, ripe for
the picking. They are a terrific size for one person and
when baked and hollowed out they make a fantastic
bowl in which to serve a creamy pumpkin risotto.

Whole Roast Pumpkin Risotto

SERVES 4

4 Golden Nugget pumpkins

Salt and pepper

100g butter

**1 litre (4 cups) chicken stock
(see page 208) or veggie stock
(see page 59)**

Oil, for frying

**1 large brown onion,
finely diced**

2 garlic cloves, finely diced

**400g (2 cups) risotto
(Arborio) rice**

500ml (2 cups) dry white wine

**60g Parmesan, finely grated,
plus extra to serve**

**Small bunch of flat-leaf parsley,
finely chopped**

Preheat your oven to 200°C.

Slice the top off the pumpkins around three-quarters of the
way up. Put the lids aside and use a spoon to scrape out
the seeds and fibrous bits from inside. Place the pumpkin on
a baking tray and season the inside with a little salt and pepper.
Drop a small knob of butter in each of the pumpkins, pop the
tops back on and slide the tray into the oven. Cook for around
35 minutes or until the flesh is tender.

Remove the pumpkins from the oven, take the lids off and use a
spoon to delicately scoop out the flesh, leaving a little on the skin
to help support the shape. Place the flesh and the hollowed-out
pumpkins and their lids to one side.

To make the risotto, pour the stock into a saucepan and bring
it to the boil. Turn the heat off and leave the pot on the stove.

Splash some oil into a deep-sided frypan and gently fry the
onion and garlic. Once the onion is translucent, add the rice
and stir it with the onion and garlic until the rice is slightly
translucent and hot to the touch. Pour in the white wine and
let it bubble away until it's almost absorbed.

There's a fair bit of debate about whether you should stir the rice
as you're cooking a risotto. I've always been a bit of a stirrer and it
hasn't gotten me into trouble yet. Pour in a ladle of the stock and
give the rice an occasional stir as it absorbs the liquid. Repeat
this until the rice is cooked and there is still some stock left to
absorb. Fold through the cooked pumpkin, the Parmesan, the
parsley and the remainder of the butter. Give it all a good beat
with a spatula to bring it together and then spoon the finished
risotto into the reserved pumpkin shells. Grate a little Parmesan
over the top, pop the lids on and serve straight away.

Pies are arguably the closest thing that we Aussies have to a national dish. We didn't invent them and we're definitely not the only culture to make them, but we've certainly taken to them with great gusto. Most of the pies consumed in this country are without a doubt beef pies, filled with a bare minimum of identifiable meat bits. However, these veggie pies are a whole different story – loaded with pumpkin, plenty of tasty spices and a hit of chilli.

Savoury Pumpkin Pies

MAKES 8 INDIVIDUAL PIES, OR 1 FAMILY-SIZED PIE

2 sheets of frozen shortcrust pastry, thawed

1.2kg pumpkin, skin and seeds removed, cut into 2cm cubes

Olive oil, for roasting and frying

Salt and pepper

2 fresh bay leaves

3 teaspoons cumin seeds, toasted

3 teaspoons coriander seeds, toasted

1 teaspoon ground cinnamon

½ teaspoon freshly grated nutmeg

1 brown onion, thinly sliced

1 mild red chilli, deseeded and finely sliced

Small bunch of flat-leaf parsley, finely chopped

2 sheets of frozen puff pastry, thawed

2 tablespoons full cream milk

2 tablespoons sesame seeds

Lightly grease eight individual pie dishes or one 30cm large dish.

Lay the shortcrust pastry sheets over the pie tins, cutting the sheets as necessary to fit. Gently press the pastry into the base of the tins, then trim any excess and pop them in the fridge until you're ready with the filling.

Preheat your oven to 170°C and line an oven tray with baking paper.

Lay the pumpkin cubes in a single layer on the oven tray. Pour over a little olive oil, season with salt and pepper and toss in a couple of bay leaves.

Lay a sheet of baking paper over the top of the pumpkin, and roll the edges of the two sheets together to make a little pumpkin parcel. Pop the tray in the oven and bake for around 15 minutes or until the pumpkin is just starting to soften. Then, whip off the top sheet of paper, crank the oven to 220°C and put the tray back in to continue cooking for another 5–10 minutes until the pumpkin is totally soft and a little crunchy around the edges.

Meanwhile, crush the cumin and coriander seeds in a mortar and pestle along with the cinnamon and nutmeg.

Heat a little oil in a frypan over a medium heat and sauté the onion and chilli for a couple of minutes until they are both soft. Add the ground spices to the pan and cook for about 2 minutes until aromatic. Remove from the heat and add to a bowl with the cooked pumpkin and parsley. Season with salt and pepper and mix together. Let the mixture cool and then spoon into the shortcrust pie bases.

Place the puff pastry sheets over the top of the filled pie shells. Trim off any excess and pinch the edges together to seal. Prick the tops with the tip of a knife or a skewer so that steam can escape while cooking, then brush a little milk over the pastry and sprinkle on the sesame seeds.

Set the oven temperature to 190°C and put the pies in to bake for around 25–30 minutes. The pastry on top should be golden and puffed, the filling steaming hot and the base firm and cooked. Serve as soon as they're cool enough to handle.

I love eating meat as much as the next guy, but
that's not to say that I need it with every single meal.
A hearty dish of spicy, slow-cooked pumpkin can
be prepared in a fraction of the time it takes to make
a stew and does a wonderful job of staving off hunger
on a cold and gloomy winter's night.

Pumpkin with Yoghurt, Mint and Slivered Almonds

SERVES 4

Oil, for frying

2 brown onions, thinly sliced

3 garlic cloves, thinly sliced

2 teaspoons ground cumin

2 teaspoons paprika

1 teaspoon coriander seeds,
toasted and ground

2 x 400g cans chopped
tomatoes

250ml (1 cup) veggie stock
(see page 59)

2 cinnamon sticks

1kg pumpkin, peeled, seeds
removed, cut into bite-sized
pieces

1 x 400g can chickpeas,
drained and well rinsed

YOGHURT DRESSING

250ml (1 cup) natural yoghurt
(see page 245)

60g (½ cup) slivered almonds,
lightly toasted

Small bunch of mint,
leaves picked

Zest of 1 lemon

Heat a deep-sided casserole dish over a medium–high heat, add a splash of oil and then sauté the onions until they are soft and just starting to turn golden, then add the garlic, cumin, paprika and coriander seeds and fry until aromatic.

Pour in the chopped tomatoes and veggie stock and then add the cinnamon sticks and pumpkin to the casserole dish. There should be just enough liquid to immerse the pumpkin – if it's a bit short top up with some water or more veggie stock.

Cover the dish with a lid but leave it slightly ajar so that steam can escape and the sauce can reduce. Bring to a simmer and cook for 20 minutes or until the pumpkin is just about soft. Add the chickpeas, stir well and continue cooking until the pumpkin is completely cooked.

To serve, remove the lid and then spoon over the yoghurt and scatter with toasted almonds, mint leaves and lemon zest. Let everyone serve themselves straight from the casserole dish, with a side of herby couscous alongside.

This recipe was shared with me by a Bega local, Bruce 'the jam man' Williamson. It's a great way to save some of the enormous summer bounty of zucchini for those winter days when the sun isn't shining quite so bright and the fireplace is cranking.

Zucchini Relish

MAKES ABOUT 750ML

1.25kg zucchini, about 10 or so, preferably a mixture of colours

2 brown onions, finely sliced

2 garlic cloves, finely sliced

2 mild red chillies, finely sliced

500ml (2 cups) apple cider vinegar

275g (1¼ cups) caster sugar

½ tablespoon celery seeds

½ tablespoon mustard seeds

½ tablespoon salt

½ tablespoon ground turmeric

¼ teaspoon ground cloves

2 tablespoons cornflour, if needed

Water, as needed

Trim the zucchini and coarsely grate them.

Put the zucchini, onion, garlic, chilli and vinegar into a large, heavy-based saucepan and bring to a boil over a medium–high heat. Add the sugar to the pan, stirring constantly to ensure the sugar is dissolved completely, and then stir in the spices. Reduce the heat to low and gently simmer for about 1 hour, uncovered, to reduce, stirring occasionally to make sure the bottom doesn't catch and burn.

After about 45–50 minutes of cooking, check the consistency of the relish. If watery bits run off a spoonful then you can use a cornflour slurry to thicken it a little. In a small bowl or cup, add some cold water to the cornflour and whisk it until it has the consistency of cream. Pour a little of the mixture into the relish and allow to cook for a minute and then check the consistency again. Keep adding a little at a time until the relish is thick and saucy. Remember, though, you're much better off adding a little at a time and getting it right than adding too much and spoiling the relish. Once you've got the consistency right, spoon the relish into sterilised jars (see page 23) and seal while still hot.

Store in a pantry cupboard for a couple of weeks to allow the flavours to develop and then enjoy up until next year's zucchini harvest.

Keep an eye out around your neighbourhood in autumn for ornamental trees laden with little red apples. A cousin *and* ancestor to the orchard apple, crab apples are widely planted for their showy displays of springtime flowers but the autumn fruit is often overlooked. More tart than the sourest cooking apple, when handled correctly crab apples make a wonderfully tangy relish that is right at home on a barbecued snag or alongside some cold cuts and cheese. If you can't lay your hands on crab apples, you can always substitute some Granny Smiths.

Crab Apple Relish

MAKES 500ML

1kg crab apples (or Granny Smith apples), peeled and cored

1 red onion, roughly chopped

2 large garlic cloves, peeled

Olive oil, for roasting

Salt and pepper

1 teaspoon cumin seeds, toasted

1 teaspoon coriander seeds, toasted

1 teaspoon ground ginger

½ teaspoon dried chilli flakes

150ml apple cider vinegar

500ml (2 cups) water

100g (½ cup) brown sugar

Preheat your oven to 150°C.

Put the apple pieces and onion onto a baking tray with the garlic and a lathering of olive oil. Season with some salt and pepper and roast in the oven for around 30 minutes, or until the fruit and veggies just start to colour.

Combine the toasted cumin and coriander seeds, ground ginger and chilli flakes in a mortar and pestle and grind to a fine consistency.

When the veg and fruit are ready transfer them to a food processor and blend along with the spice mix, the apple cider vinegar and the 2 cups of water. Transfer the ingredients to a heavy-based saucepan, add the sugar, give it a good stir and gently bring to a simmer. Continue cooking for 45 minutes, by which stage the relish will have thickened and darkened a little in colour.

Check the seasoning and transfer into sterilised jars (see page 23). Pop a label on each jar and store the relish in your pantry for up to a year. You can use it immediately, though the depth of flavour will increase over time.

Hugh made this salsa to go with the spit-roast pig he cooked during a visit to the farm. For this recipe, you need the Fuyu variety of persimmon – sometimes also called a Sharon fruit. Squat and chunky, it has the advantage of being tasty and toothsome even if it is only just ripe. They'll get sweeter and more tender if stored at room temperature. The more astringent type of persimmon (usually the Hachiya variety) is mouth-puckeringly tart when under-ripe and can't be enjoyed until it's been allowed to soften to the point of near-collapse.

As well as a flavour-packed accompaniment to spit-roast pork (see pages 184–5), this is a great salsa to serve with pulled pork or roast lamb. It also goes brilliantly with good old butcher's bangers or pork chops. It's easy to scale the recipe up if you're feeding a crowd.

Hugh's Persimmon Coriander Salsa

SERVES 4–6

250g of Fuyu persimmons

30g bunch of coriander, leaves picked and chopped

Juice of 1 lime

1 tablespoon extra-virgin olive oil

Salt and pepper

Dice the persimmons finely, discarding their tough leafy tops. Put them in a bowl and add all the other ingredients. Stir well, then taste and adjust the seasoning if necessary.

For a variation, use the Hachiya variety, peeled and diced, omit the coriander and add a finely chopped shallot and a finely sliced red chilli to the recipe.

I'm all for delayed gratification, but sometimes you just need something straight away. There's plenty of opportunity to enjoy summer's slow-cooked pickles, relishes and chutneys in the cooler months of the year, but when it's high summer and there is a glut of cucumbers in the garden, I like to throw together this quick pickle. By the time I've popped it in the fridge to cool down and had a quick poke around the garden, it's ready to go with some cold meat and bitey cheese for lunch.

Quick Cucumber Pickle

MAKES 1½ LITRES

750ml (3 cups) apple cider vinegar

330g (1½ cups) caster sugar

2 teaspoons salt

½ teaspoon mustard seeds

½ teaspoon celery seeds

¼ teaspoon ground turmeric

4 Lebanese cucumbers, topped, tailed and cut into thin slices

Small bunch of fresh fennel fronds

In a medium saucepan, combine the vinegar, sugar, salt, mustard seeds, celery seeds and ground turmeric. Bring to a boil, stirring to dissolve the sugar.

Arrange the sliced cucumbers and fennel fronds in sterilised jars (see page 23) and then pour the hot brine in on top. Seal the jars straight away and pop them in the fridge to cool. Use within two weeks.

FISH

Of all the sources of wild protein, fish is without a doubt the most accessible to the average punter and it's still a staple source of animal protein for many communities around the world. While we're a long way from depending on fish for survival here in Australia, a couple of hours a week spent working our abundant waterways can still provide you with a healthy, delicious and economical way of feeding your family.

When it comes to places to wet a line, we really are spoilt for choice. We're surrounded by 35,000km of coastline studded with 738 estuaries, as well as countless rivers and dams that play host to roughly 5000 species of fish, a respectable chunk of which are edible. Add to that a cornucopia of edible molluscs and crustaceans and it's clear that when it comes to seafood and the kitchen, we really do live in the lucky country.

The United Nations Food and Agriculture Organization (FAO) estimates that the average Aussie eats around 25kg of seafood every year. Given our coastline and waterways, and our relatively small population, you would think that the majority of the seafood that we consume would come from Australian waters. I was shocked to find that almost three-quarters of the seafood that we eat is imported and that Australians are more likely to opt for something that has been tinned or frozen overseas and then shipped here than the fresh local product. I know what I'd prefer if I had a choice between a tasteless fillet of catfish from a muddy river in South East Asia or a quiveringly fresh fillet of flathead from my local waterway. While not everyone has the time, means or inclination to chase their own fishy dinner, if you do, there are plenty of species that can be sustainably caught with minimal equipment and a bit of know-how.

If you're new to the whole fishing experience then it's a good idea to seek the advice of a friend who fishes or visit your local tackle shop to find out what you'll need to get started and a few tips about what's biting and where. A simple rod and reel combo, some hooks, swivels, sinkers and bait will have you cheaply equipped to start putting some fresh fish on the dinner table. Don't get too carried away with kit, though – just remember that fish don't care how expensive your fishing rod is, they're just looking for a feed. Before you head out make sure that you check with the relevant authorities about licensing requirements and size and bag limits.

While you can never be certain what fish you'll encounter, or of catching something at all for that matter, it does pay to head out with a plan. Familiarising yourself with a few key species will greatly increase your chances of heading home with a feed instead of an empty bucket. Some – like flathead, trout and prawns – are familiar fare at the local fishmonger, but when it comes to freshness and satisfaction, catching them yourself is a different kettle of fish. Other species are viewed as having little economic or culinary value so they'll rarely grace the crushed ice of the fishmonger's display and the only way to experience their flavour will be to haul them in yourself. Here's a quick list of my favourite fish to chase, along with a few saltwater delicacies that are well worth the effort of seeking out.

SALTWATER SPECIES

Yellowfin Bream: Found in estuaries and around rocky headlands on beaches. Fish them on the incoming tide, with worms, prawns or small fish for bait. Bream has a tasty, firm white flesh that is sweet and delicate, and it's very versatile in the kitchen.

Flathead: There are more than three dozen species of flathead, also known as flatties or lizards, found in Australian waters. To find flathead, look for sandy or muddy bottoms in estuaries and close to the coast; they're an ambush predator and lie camouflaged until a likely victim swims by. For bait use worms, prawns, pilchards or crabs. Flathead are an excellent eating fish and a couple of firm, white fillets are perfect for a serve of fish and chips.

Australian Salmon: Also known as cocky salmon, this fish isn't actually a salmon at all, but nonetheless it's a fantastic sporting fish and a massively underrated table fish. The best place to find Aussie salmon is in large schools in deep gutters along a beach in the early morning, or from the late afternoon into the night. For bait try pilchards, whitebait, squid or beach worms. When you land an Aussie salmon, bleed it straight away to improve the flavour. The flesh is oily and robust and is wonderful baked, fried or even raw. Don't let all the bad press about this fish put you off – treated right and eaten fresh it's delicious!

Sea Mullet: Another fish that is unfortunately perceived as being second rate, the mullet – and its roe – are welcome in my kitchen any time. The best time to chase mullet is during their spawning migration, which happens towards the end of autumn and in early winter. The fish are laden with roe and congregate in large

schools along the sandy bottoms of calm beaches and bays. Despite their hefty size, they can be caught using just a light tackle and small hooks. Get the school interested by throwing in some small chunks of bread as berley, then bait a hook that's set about 20cm below a small float with some bread dough and delicately cast to the edge of the school. Once you've landed a fish, bleed, gut and clean it straight away, reserving the roe if there is any. Mullet have flavoursome, oily flesh that is delicious lightly floured and fried or stuffed and roasted whole. The closer to the ocean that you catch your fish, the better the flavour will be. Mullet that are caught at the top of estuaries or in tributaries tend to have a muddier flavour that reflects the water that they have been feeding in.

FRESHWATER SPECIES

Trout: Rainbow, Brown and Brook trout can be found in the cold-water rivers and lakes of the Australian Alps and Tasmania. Trout are an invasive species that have a significant impact on native fish stocks and fresh water ecologies; fortunately for us hungry conservationists, they also make great eating. Trout can be caught on fly lures, spinners and bait such as garden worms, cockroaches, crickets and grasshoppers. Try casting around deep holes, back eddies and anywhere that there is a little shelter that the trout can use to ambush passing fish. Trout fishing is also subject to seasonal closures so check with the local authorities before heading out.

MOLLUSCS, CRUSTACEANS AND ECHINODERMS

Prawns: These tasty crustaceans have embedded themselves in our summer cooking culture, and rightfully so. The sweet white flesh is a special treat with little more than a dollop of mayo and a squeeze of lemon juice. If you have the time, I highly recommend you try catching your own. All you'll need is a waterproof light source (purpose-made prawning lights are available from most tackle shops), a fine net and a bucket for your haul. Pick a night around the new moon and head out to a coastal lake or river after dark. Start as close to the river mouth or the edge of the lake as possible and wade along the shallows using the light to spot the prawns. Once you get your eye in, spotting them is a piece of cake and an hour spent in the water usually yields enough for a decent feed. Before cooking the prawns plunge them into a bucket of ice water for 10 minutes or so to sedate them. To cook the prawns

I like to give them a toss in a little seasoned cornflour and then deep-fry them whole – they're delicious head, shells and all!

Blue Mussels: Found in intertidal areas anchored to things like rocks, pylons and mooring chains. They live between the low-tide mark and a depth of around 10m and can be easily removed by hand as long as you can get to them. So all you really need to pluck off a feed of these tasty bivalves is a dive mask and a catch bag. I love tossing a couple of handfuls of mussels over a fire on the beach and eating them straight from the shell. Remember, though, that mussels are filter feeders and are a reflection of the health of a waterway. If you want to forage for your own, try to find a waterway that is free from run-off and pollution, preferably in an undeveloped area.

Native Oysters: Also known as mud oysters or angasi oysters, these are native to the coastal fringe of southern Australia. They can be found sitting by themselves, settled into the silty bottom of coastal lakes and estuaries from knee-deep water to a depth of 30m. Half an hour spent wading the shallows in bare feet, looking with both your eyes and your feet, will usually be enough to fill an empty bucket, or belly.

Sea Urchins: Found in abundance, hidden in the crevices of rocky reef systems and headlands around the south-east of the country. Urchins are prized for their salty roe and are easily foraged off the rocks – all you need is a dive mask and catch bag. The spines can be a little troublesome, so a nice thick glove is also a good bit of kit unless, of course, you're a steel-handed He-Man.

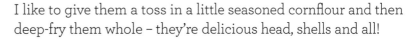

Octopus: Rarely sought by fishermen in Australia but a staple in Mediterranean countries like Greece. Octopuses can be found lurking in their rocky lairs in estuaries and around headlands. The octopuses themselves can be difficult to spot but their lairs can be easily identified by the scattering of discarded shells from previous meals. A dive mask and a hand spear are all the equipment you'll need. Once the octopus has been speared, dispatch it quickly by putting two fingers into the hood behind the head and then turn it inside out.

Sardine Escabeche

SERVES 4

12 butterflied sardines

Salt and pepper

Oil, for frying

Extra-virgin olive oil, for
drizzling

1 small brown onion,
thinly sliced

1 carrot, thinly sliced

2 sprigs of thyme

3 bay leaves

2 garlic cloves,
thinly sliced

1 mild red chilli,
thinly sliced

250ml (1 cup) white wine

Juice of 2 oranges

Pinch of saffron threads

Splash of white wine vinegar

Flat-leaf parsley, finely chopped

Season the sardine fillets with salt and pepper and then fry,
skin-side down, in a little oil in a large frypan over a medium
heat. As soon as the skin is golden and crispy remove the fillets
from the heat and arrange in a single layer in a deep-sided dish.
Drizzle over a little extra-virgin olive oil.

Put the onion, carrot, thyme, bay leaves, garlic and chilli and
a little more oil in the pan on a low heat and cook for a few
minutes until softened. Add the white wine, orange juice and
saffron to the pan and then add just enough white wine vinegar
to give the sauce a bit of tang. Bring it all to the boil and
simmer for 5 minutes, then remove from the heat, adjust the
seasoning and pour over the sardine fillets. Cover the dish
and let it stand and infuse in the fridge for an hour.

To finish, spoon onto serving plates and sprinkle with parsley.
Serve cold, with crusty white bread.

Australian salmon is not really salmon at all. It's actually more closely related to herring, but was named by early settlers who, nostalgic for home perhaps, thought it looked rather salmon-y. It doesn't have a great reputation as an eating fish, but like me Hugh found it delicious – firm, rich and full flavoured.

If you can't get it from your fishmonger, this dish is fantastic with bream, line-caught bonito or sea mullet and most other firm-fleshed sea fish.

Hugh's Australian Salmon Tartare

SERVES 4 AS A STARTER

A few young nasturtium leaves (or a handful of other peppery leaves such as rocket or watercress)

300g Australian salmon fillet, skin removed

Salt and pepper

Extra-virgin olive oil

Small bunch of chives, chopped

6 nasturtium capers or 2 teaspoons regular baby capers, rinsed and chopped

A squeeze of lemon juice

More nasturtium leaves, to serve

A few nasturtium flowers or extra chopped chives (optional), to serve

Shred the nasturtium leaves by rolling them into tight little 'cigars' then slicing across them to form thin shreds. If you're using other leaves, just chop them roughly. Set aside.

Place the fish on a board and check for pin bones, prising out any you find with tweezers. With your knife at an angle, cut the fillet across the grain into thin (3–5mm) slices. Cutting across, rather than along, the muscle fibres will give you rectangular slices of fillet to work with rather than long, tapering bits, and make for a neater dice. Cut each slice into long ribbons, then cut across the ribbons to form small dice. Put the diced fish into a bowl and season with salt, pepper and a good trickle of olive oil.

Stir a good couple of pinches each of shredded nasturtium leaves, chives and capers into the salmon. Give the mixture a spritz of lemon juice. Taste and add more of any of the flavourings or seasonings you think are needed.

To serve, put spoonfuls of the fish mixture onto individual nasturtium leaves (or thin slices of toasted sourdough loaf, pages 218–19) and finish with a nasturtium petal – or with a few more chives.

Where I live, on the south coast of New South Wales, there is a huge amount of recreational game fishing. Boats will find a school of bonito and land a couple of these fish to use as bait for more alluring sport fish, like marlin and Yellowfin tuna. Personally, I head straight back to shore as soon as I've landed a bonito – why troll all day when you've already bagged a great feed? Bonito is fast growing and quick to mature, making it an excellent, sustainable alternative to the more glamorous members of the tuna family. If you can't catch one for yourself, ask your fishmonger for line-caught bonito. Its oily flesh is nutritious, versatile and excellent eaten raw, and a few simple additions can quickly transform the fillets into a healthy light meal.

Raw Bonito Salad

SERVES 8

1 bonito, bled, cleaned and filleted with the skin and bloodline removed

1 bunch small red radishes

2cm piece horseradish

Small bunch of wood sorrel leaves and flowers (or some finely chopped flat-leaf parsley)

2 lemons

Chill the two bonito fillets so that they are nice and firm. Cut each fillet into two long strips, and then with your knife on a slight angle cut across the strips to create thin slices about 3mm thick. Arrange on a big serving platter.

Using a mandolin or a very sharp knife, thinly slice the radishes and arrange over the fish slices. Using a zester, grate the horseradish over the top of everything and then scatter over the wood sorrel leaves.

Finish off by squeezing lemon juice over the top and enjoy straight away.

Once known as poor man's caviar, bottarga is the salted and cured roe of the grey (sea) mullet and has been a culinary stalwart around the Mediterranean for centuries. The salting process transforms the delicate egg sac into a hard slab of fishy deliciousness which, stored correctly, will last until next year's mullet run. Thinly sliced or grated bottarga adds a wonderful, salty complexity to simple dishes like pasta, eggs and braised beans.

Mullet Roe Bottarga

4 mullet roe, sacs intact

Cooking salt

Generously cover the bottom of a deep-sided dish with salt and lay the mullet roe on top.

Sprinkle more salt over, making sure that the surface of the roe is evenly covered. Cover and place the tray in the refrigerator. Every day remove the tray, pour off any liquid that has been drawn out of the roe and add fresh salt. Repeat this process for about a week or until the roe feels firm to the touch.

You can use this bottarga straight away, though I prefer to cure it further by hanging it uncovered in a cool, airy place for a fortnight. Make a hole in it with a skewer and hang it up with some string. After that, tightly wrap the bottarga in cling film and store it in the fridge for up to a year.

Spaghetti with Bottarga

SERVES 4

400g dried spaghetti

Olive oil, for frying

4 garlic cloves, finely chopped

2 anchovy fillets in oil, drained and finely chopped

1 mild red chilli, thinly sliced

Small bunch of flat-leaf parsley leaves, finely chopped

Salt and pepper

Zest and juice of 1 lemon

Bottarga

Bring a pot of lightly salted water to the boil, and cook the spaghetti until al dente.

While the spaghetti is cooking heat a good glug of olive oil in a pan over a low–medium heat. Add the chopped garlic, anchovy fillets and chilli to the pan and stir-fry until they just start to become fragrant.

Thoroughly drain the cooked pasta and add it to the pan along with the parsley. Season with salt and pepper and then transfer into bowls. Add a little lemon zest to each bowl as well as some juice and finish by using a microplane to finely grate a generous amount of the bottarga over the top.

Mullet is a fish we should all be eating more often. It may not be the most glamourous fish in the fishmonger's cabinet, but when it's been sea run it has a subtle, delicious flavour. The rich, oily flesh is perfect for chargrilling on a barbecue, and pairing it with a salty, vinegary salad shows just what a prime eating fish it is. Try it. Any doubts you have will be dispelled.

Chargrilled Grey Mullet with Tomato and Green Capsicum Salad

SERVES 4

A chunk of stale bread

4 ripe tomatoes, diced

Extra-virgin olive oil

Salt and pepper

1 green capsicum, seeds removed, halved and finely sliced

1 red onion, finely sliced

80g (½ cup) pitted green olives, roughly chopped

Small bunch of flat-leaf parsley, finely chopped

Red wine vinegar

Oil, for frying

4 x 200g mullet fillets, skin on

Lemon cheeks, to serve

Tear the stale bread up into bite-sized chunks and add to a mixing bowl. Toss in the tomatoes, drizzle in a little extra-virgin olive oil, season liberally with salt and pepper and give the whole thing a good mix. Add the finely sliced capsicum, the onion, green olives and parsley to the bowl. Toss it all together with a little splash of red wine vinegar. Check the seasoning, adding more oil/vinegar/salt/pepper to taste and then put to one side.

Heat a chargrill to a medium–high heat. Drizzle a little oil over both sides of the mullet fillets and season well with salt. Cook the fillets skin-side down for a couple of minutes or until the skin is crispy. Turn the fillets and cook for a further minute and then remove from the heat.

Serve with the tomato salad and big cheeks of lemon.

Bream can be found around most of the Australian coastline, taking shelter around bridge pylons, oyster leases, jetties and rocky headlands. It has a delicious, firm white flesh and a delicate skin that makes it perfect for panfrying. This simple preparation offers a great balance of flavours, with the sweetness of the fish, the nuttiness of the brown butter, the fresh parsley and the zing of the lemon all coming together in a classic sauce.

Panfried Bream with Lemon and Capers

SERVES 2

Oil, for frying

1 Black or Yellowfin bream (about 1kg), filleted, skin on

1 teaspoon butter

Small handful of baby capers

Juice of 1 lemon

Small handful of flat-leaf parsley, roughly chopped

Drizzle a little oil into a frypan on a medium–high heat. As soon as the oil starts to shimmer and very lightly smoke, add the fillets, skin-side down. Cook the fillets for a couple of minutes until the skin is brown and crispy.

Delicately turn the fish and then add the butter and capers to the pan. As soon as the butter has melted and starts to foam spoon it over the fish and keep doing so until the fish is just about cooked and the butter has started to brown. This should only take a minute or two. Remove from the heat and add the lemon juice and parsley.

Place the cooked fillets on a plate and drizzle over the brown butter. Serve with a salad of sweet leafy greens (such as butter lettuce) and crisp fennel.

Trout has a lovely, fine skin and sweet, oily flesh that is ideal for panfrying. Couple it with a generous bowl of sweet, braised peas and you've got a quick but seriously tasty meal. This dish will go down a treat in front of a roaring fire after a long day wading in alpine streams.

Panfried Trout with Braised Peas

SERVES 4

200g piece of speck, cut into batons

Oil, for frying

1 small brown onion, finely sliced

2 garlic cloves, minced

250ml (1 cup) chicken stock (see page 208)

310g (2 cups) podded green peas

4 trout fillets, skin on

Salt and pepper

Knob of butter

Small bunch of mint, finely chopped

1 lemon

60g (½ cup) slivered almonds, toasted

Heat a deep-sided frypan over a medium–high heat. Fry the speck in a little oil, stirring until it is nicely coloured all over.

Next, add the onion and garlic and cook until the onion begins to soften and the garlic becomes aromatic. Pour in the chicken stock and bring to the boil, then as soon as it's bubbling away add the peas.

While the peas are cooking you can cook your trout fillets. Heat a second pan over a medium heat and season the fillets lightly with salt and pepper. Cook the fillets skin-side down until the skin is brown and crispy and then turn and cook for only a few seconds on the other side.

At the same time, simmer the peas until the stock is reduced and they are just cooked. Toss in the knob of butter and swirl the pan until the butter has emulsified with the chicken stock to make a creamy sauce. Add the chopped mint to the pan, give it one more swirl and then check the seasoning, finishing with a big squeeze of lemon juice.

Transfer the trout fillets to serving plates and top with the buttery, braised peas and toasted almonds.

People have been smoking fish for as long as they've been catching them. I particularly enjoy smoking my own trout – the rich, fatty flesh seems to absorb the subtle smoky flavour perfectly. You can build your own hot smoker at home and it's not a great stretch to go a little further and build your own cold smoker. Smoked trout is a versatile ingredient to have in the fridge – it can give a lift to egg dishes, add a smoky tang to a salad, make beautiful rillettes or add depth to a pasta. Wild-caught trout definitely tastes the best, but if you don't have the chance to flick a fly in a trout stream a farmed trout will still smoke very nicely.

Smoked Trout

MAKES 2 SMOKED TROUT

About 150g (½ cup) cooking salt

About 100g (½ cup) brown sugar

Note: The exact measurement isn't important, as long as there are roughly equal proportions of salt and sugar.

2 x 1kg Rainbow, Brook or Brown trout, cleaned and skin removed (and filleted, if preferred)

You can smoke either whole fish or fillets – both produce wonderful results. Mix the salt and sugar together to form a dry rub, then massage it into every part of the fish. Place the fish on a deep-sided baking tray, cover it with cling film and leave it in the fridge for a couple of hours. This curing process helps season the flesh while removing excess moisture; it also leaves the surface with a tack that helps the smoke to adhere. The curing takes a fair while, so I like to prepare my fish in the afternoon and leave it in the fridge overnight.

The next morning, thoroughly rinse the trout with cold water to remove the curing rub. Now your fish is ready to smoke. There are two different methods: hot smoking, which is quick and cooks the fish as well as imparting a smoky flavour, and cold smoking, which takes significantly longer, doesn't cook the fish and helps to preserve the flesh for a lot longer. Both methods use the same fuel source for the smoke: woodchips. There are tonnes of different types of smoking chips available from hardware and fishing stores. I like to use dried banksia seedpods because they grow in abundance around the coastal fringe of Australia, they take very little preparation, they produce a mild, flavoursome smoke and most importantly – they're free.

HOT SMOKING

Hot smoking is as simple as heating your chips until they smoke, then sealing the smoking chips and the fish in a vessel such as a wok or an old biscuit tin, which both make perfect hot smokers.

First make a thin foil vessel to hold your smoking chips. Fold a 30cm piece of foil in half and roll each edge in a little towards the centre. Place the smoking chips inside it and then transfer it

into your chosen smoker. On a gas burner in the kitchen or over the coals of a fire, heat your smoker until the chips begin to smoulder. Place a wire rack over the smouldering chips, place the fish on the rack and seal the container with its lid. If you're using a wok, use the lid from a large saucepan. Make sure that there is enough heat underneath the smoker to keep the chips smouldering and after 15 minutes or so the fish will be cooked through and seasoned with a delicious smoky flavour. You can eat the fish straight away or wrap it and store it in the fridge for a couple of days.

COLD SMOKING

For cold smoking you need to separate the smoking chamber from the source of the smoke and the heat that it produces. I've converted an old fridge and an old slow-combustion fireplace into a great little cold smoker.

First I build a fire in the old fireplace and then let it burn down to coals. Then I place a metal tray over the fire and lay out my smoking chips. The smoke is piped through an old bucket full of ice and then into the bottom of the fridge. A makeshift chimney in the top of the fridge draws the smoke from the firebox, over the fish and out the top. I usually just lay the whole fish on the shelves of the fridge and shut the door so that the smoke can work its magic.

Cold smoking takes around 8 hours, so make sure that you keep the fire ticking away just enough to keep the chips smouldering. You'll also have to top up the chips as they burn down. Once the trout is ready it will be firm to the touch and yellowed by the smoke. Enjoy thin slices straight away or keep it wrapped in the fridge for up to a month.

Whole Kingfish
with Lemongrass and Thyme

SERVES 10

2 lemongrass stalks

**Small bunch of thyme,
leaves picked – keep the stems**

2 lemons, zested and then sliced

150g (½ cup) salt

1 x 5kg kingfish, cleaned

Olive oil, for drizzling

Prepare the lemongrass by removing the tough outer leaves, giving the pale part a good whack using the side of a knife and then thinly slicing it. Add the thyme leaves and lemon zest to a mortar along with the lemongrass and the salt and pound with a pestle until you have an aromatic, salty rub.

Preheat the barbecue to a medium heat.

Lay the fish out on a big, clean board. Using a sharp knife, lightly score the flesh on both sides and then massage the salt rub all over, inside and out. Stuff the lemon slices into the belly cavity along with the thyme stems. Give the whole fish a good drizzling of olive oil and then wrap it up in foil, twice. Gently transfer to the warmed barbecue plate or grill.

The fish will take around 10 minutes on each side. You can tell if it's cooked by unrolling a bit of the foil and flaking back a little flesh on the thickest part of the fish. If the flesh is moist and flaky all the way to the bone the fish is done; if it is still firm and opaque roll the foil back up and keep cooking for a few minutes more.

Transfer to a serving platter, open up the foil, and break and serve by flaking apart the fillets with a couple of forks. Start with the top fillet, then lift out the skeleton and finish off the second. Add a crunchy salad and a dollop of mayo and everyone can tuck in.

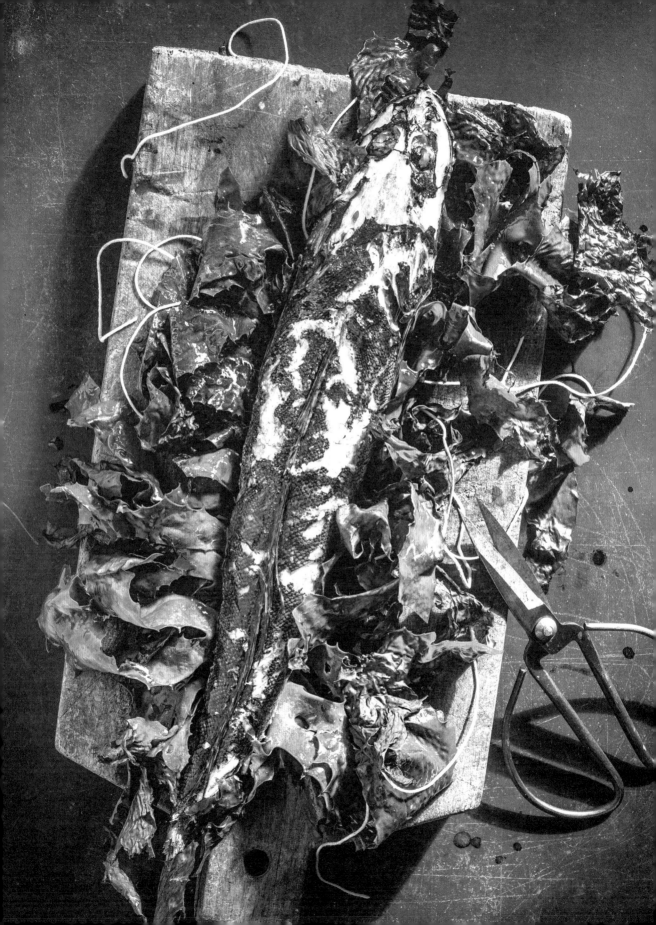

Flathead, otherwise known as flatties or lizards, live in abundance in the numerous waterways of the New South Wales south coast and they can be found in some form or another in pretty much every salty waterway around Australia. Chances are that if you've only caught one fish in your life, you've caught a flathead. The tasty white flesh means that it is welcome in any kitchen or on any barbecue, whether it's battered and fried, grilled or roasted whole.

For something a little different I like to visit my local beach after a bit of swell has washed up some fresh leather kelp, which I use to wrap and steam the fish in, imparting a delicious salty note. If you don't have any kelp, a baking-paper parcel will work fine — but just remember to add a little salt.

Flathead Steamed in Seaweed

SERVES 2

1 whole flathead, cleaned

Pepper

Olive oil

Fresh leather kelp (enough to wrap the fish)

Lemon wedges, to serve

Preheat your oven to 180°C.

Season your fish with pepper and olive oil. This would be the only time that I wouldn't recommend seasoning your fish with salt before cooking it, as the kelp will impart its own saltiness.

Lay the leaves of kelp over a chopping board with its long side facing you. Run the leaves perpendicularly away from you to ensure even wrapping, making sure that the chopping board is well covered. Place your fish on top of the kelp and roll it up to make a seaweedy parcel. This can be a little tricky so don't despair if there are a couple of gaps. If the seaweed won't stay in place you can secure the parcel by binding it with kitchen twine. Place the fish on an oiled oven tray and bake for about 30 minutes. The lengthy baking time allows the heat to penetrate the kelp.

The cooking time will vary according to the size and/or type of fish you are baking. You can check the fish after 15 minutes or so (or after 10 minutes if you're using baking paper) by either pulling apart the wrapping slightly, or by piercing with a skewer. If you are pulling apart the wrapping, then the flesh should be opaque. If you are piercing with a skewer, the skewer should pierce the wrapping and the fish to the bone without resistance.

When the fish is cooked, take it out of the oven and break open the seaweed parcel to reveal the fish within. Serve with wedges of lemon and a crunchy garden salad.

After a long day fishing there are few things more satisfying
than a couple of pieces of freshly caught fish in a crispy
batter with a fistful of golden chips – it's one of the culinary
world's great pairings. The moist, white flesh of a flathead
tail is perfect for wrapping in batter and frying, though
whiting, tailor and bream all make excellent substitutes.
Avoid waxy potatoes – instead, search out floury types,
such as King Edward, Desiree, Royal Blue and Sebago.

Fish and Chips

SERVES 4

CHIPS

5 medium potatoes, scrubbed

**Canola oil (or 1 tablespoon
duck fat, melted – see page 205)**

Salt flakes

TARTARE

**2 quantities homemade mayo
(see page 38; save the whites
for the batter) or 250ml (1 cup)
of store-bought mayo**

**3 small, sweet pickled gherkins,
finely chopped**

**1 tablespoon capers, finely
chopped**

1 French shallot, finely diced

Small bunch of dill, finely chopped

Zest of 1 lemon

Salt and pepper

BATTER

100g self-raising flour

100g cornflour

Pinch of salt

2 free-range egg whites

**250ml (1 cup) cold,
sparkling water**

**1 litre (4 cups) rice bran oil
(or similar), for deep-frying**

Plain flour, seasoned, for dusting

8 x 20cm flathead tail fillets

Lemon wedges, to serve

Preheat the oven to 210°C.

Pop your spuds into a pot filled with cold, lightly salted water.
Heat the water to a gentle simmer and cook until the potato just
begins to yield when prodded with a knife tip (about 15 minutes).
Drain the potatoes and return to the pot to let them steam for a
minute or so to really dry out. Then cut them into chips when cool
enough to handle.

Transfer the chips to a warm roasting tray and drizzle over some
canola oil, or better yet, a big tablespoon of melted duck fat. Give
the tray a good shake, rolling the chips around until evenly covered
in oil. Season generously with some salt flakes and pop in the oven.
Give the tray a shake every 5 minutes or so, so that the chips
don't stick to the bottom and they cook evenly. They'll take about
20–25 minutes. They're done when they are golden and crispy.

While the chips are cooking, prepare the tartare sauce.

For the tartare, whip up some mayo (or a cup of store-bought stuff
is fine). Fold through the gherkins, capers, shallot and dill, add the
lemon zest and check the seasoning.

To prepare the batter, sift the flours into a large bowl and add a
pinch of salt. Whisk the egg whites in a bowl until they start to
get bubbly and thicken slightly. Slowly pour the sparkling water
into the flours and whisk to form a smooth batter. Gently fold in
the egg whites and set the batter to one side.

In a large, heavy-based saucepan, heat the frying oil to 180°C. If you
don't have a probe thermometer, when the oil is hot enough a tiny
amount of batter spooned into the pan will bubble up straight away.

Lightly dust the fillets in seasoned flour and then drag them through
the batter until nicely coated. Quickly transfer them to the hot oil,
VERY carefully dragging the fillet through the oil so a crust begins
to form before letting go. Fry in two batches to avoid overcooking.
Remove when crunchy and golden and drain off excess oil.

Serve with the crispy chips, the tartare and lemon wedges, and
sprinkle on more salt, if desired.

On moonless nights, in the warmer months, the
estuaries around where I live run with delicious little
school prawns. An evening spent with a flashlight and a
fine net can easily bag a feed for four. Lightly coated in
cornflour and quickly fried whole these tiny prawns
make the ultimate summer beer snack. The chilli and
lime add an extra kick and zing that really gets your
mouth watering.

Crunchy Whole School Prawns with Lime and Chilli

SERVES 4

750g raw school prawns, unpeeled

Zest of 2 limes

2 tablespoons salt flakes, plus extra

125g (1 cup) cornflour or tapioca flour

375ml rice bran oil (or similar), plus extra, for deep-frying

Dried chilli flakes and lime wedges, to serve

Rinse the school prawns to give them a good clean and to get rid of any sand or grit. If using live prawns, fill a bucket with water and ice and put the prawns in until they are sedated (this should take around 10 minutes). Drain the prawns and pat dry with kitchen paper towel.

Add the lime zest and 1 tablespoon of the salt to the cornflour or tapioca flour and toss to combine.

Heat the oil to 180°C in a large, heavy-based saucepan.

To test if the oil is at the right temperature, toss one prawn in the flour mix and then fry. It should bubble straight away and turn golden in around a minute. Working in three or four batches, toss the prawns in the flour mix, shake off any excess and cook until crisp and golden. Drain on paper towel and repeat with the remaining prawns, adding a little more oil as needed.

Sprinkle more salt flakes, chilli flakes and a squeeze of lime juice over the top of the hot prawns and enjoy immediately.

Yabbies are an Aussie favourite and this recipe is
just right for the smaller yabbies found in dams and
waterways. The kaffir in the mayonnaise adds a subtle,
perfumed citrus flavour.

Beer-battered Tempura Yabbies with Kaffir Lime Mayonnaise

SERVES 4 AS A SNACK

MAYONNAISE

2 free-range egg yolks

2 teaspoons white wine vinegar

Pinch of salt

200ml rice bran oil (you can add a little olive oil if you like but I would steer clear of a mayonnaise made entirely with olive oil, as the flavour will be overpowering)

2 kaffir lime leaves, very finely chopped

1 teaspoon cold water, if needed

YABBIES

10 yabbies, de-veined

90g (½ cup) rice flour

75g (½ cup) plain flour

250ml (1 cup) very cold beer

1 teaspoon salt

500ml (2 cups) rice bran oil (or similar), for deep-frying

First off, make the mayonnaise by whisking the egg yolks, vinegar and salt together in a bowl. Keep whisking while you steadily pour in a stream of oil. The oil will emulsify with the egg yolks, thickening the mixture into a creamy mayonnaise. It should be thick enough to momentarily hold a peak when you remove the whisk. If you add too much oil you can split your mayonnaise. If this happens, don't despair, you can always add a teaspoon of cold water to help bring it back together. Once you have the right consistency stir through the kaffir lime and taste, adjusting for salt and acidity. A good mayo should be richly flavoured and have a nice acidy tang.

To prepare the yabbies, chill them in a bucket of icy water to send them into a hibernation-like state. Once they're sedated you can dispatch them by driving the tip of a knife through the centre of the head. Then separate the tail from the head and carefully peel back the shell from around the tail meat like you would a prawn. I leave the tail fins intact as they make a useful handle for dangling the battered tails in oil to begin the cooking.

Combine the flours in a bowl and whisk in the beer until smooth, then whisk in the salt.

In a large, heavy-based saucepan heat the rice bran oil to 180°C. If you don't have a thermometer, drop a little bit of the batter in. If it sizzles and browns within 10 seconds, you're good to go.

Grab one of the shelled tails in each hand, drag the tails through the batter to coat completely and gently shake off any excess. Still holding the fins, drag the battered tails back and forth through the hot oil being VERY careful not to burn your fingers. This helps the batter to form an initial crust and prevents it from sticking to the bottom of the pan. Fry in batches of four or five so the first yabbies don't overcook while you're busy battering the next ones. After about 2–3 minutes the batter will be golden brown and the yabbie tails will be cooked.

Use a set of tongs or a slotted spoon to transfer the yabbies onto some paper towel to drain off any excess oil. Working quickly, repeat until all tails are cooked. Season with a little salt and serve with the creamy kaffir lime mayonnaise.

Hunting for the odd crayfish or two around the rocky
headlands of the New South Wales south coast is one
of my favourite things to do in the water. You don't
have to be the world's best free diver to get to the
depths that crays live but you do have to have a sharp
eye and a quick hand to pull them from their lairs.
As with so many foods, I find that to really appreciate
the delicate flavour you don't have to use a great deal
of culinary wizardry. A cray that's been cut in half and
roasted over a bed of coals on the beach and enjoyed
with a cold, crisp beer is absolute heaven to me. If you
capture the crayfish yourself or purchase them live, be
sure to kill them humanely. The soft green substance
found in the body cavity is known as tomalley and it
has a magnificent salty, crustacean flavour. It can be
scooped out and folded through a mayonnaise.

Grilled Crayfish with Tomalley Mayonnaise

SERVES 2

2 small or 1 large raw crayfish

Salt and pepper

50g butter, cut into slices, plus extra, melted

Lemon, to serve

TOMALLEY MAYONNAISE

Fresh tomalley from the cray

1 quantity homemade mayonnaise (see page 38) or 125ml (½ cup) store-bought mayonnaise

Prepare your crayfish by chilling them in a bucket of icy water for 10 minutes until they are sedated. Using the point of a large, sturdy, sharp knife, and with the cutting edge of the blade facing away from you, pierce the centre of the carapace (head). To prepare them for cooking, split them in half lengthways, and remove the intestine and the coral. Scoop out the soft green tomalley to use in the mayonnaise.

To make the mayonnaise, stir the tomalley gently through the mayo and set aside until the cray is cooked.

Get a small cooking fire going until you have a good bed of coals, then place a barbecue grate over the top (if you don't have a fire or charcoal grill, a gas barbecue will do just fine). Season the crays with salt and pepper and lay the slices of butter on the flesh. Place the halves shell-side down on the grate and grill the crays until the shells are bright red and the flesh is still translucent. This should take around 10–15 minutes over a gentle bed of coals. Baste the cray with more butter as it's grilling. You can turn your cray flesh-side down on the grate for a minute if you like your seafood well done. Don't leave it for too long, however, or the flesh will be overcooked.

When the crayfish is ready allow it to rest for a couple of minutes before serving. Spoon the tomalley mayo into a small dish or the head cavities, and dress the crayfish with salt, pepper and a squeeze of lemon.

Octopus, like other cephalopods, becomes beautifully tender if you cook it gently and slowly. In this recipe, Hugh has also added some delicious, caramelised flavours by grilling the cooked octopus flesh. Combined with a fragrant, aromatic dressing, it makes for a really spectacular salad. You can use the same dressing and salad ingredients to make a great chargrilled squid salad – and there's no need to pre-cook the squid.

Hugh's Grilled Octopus Salad with Lemongrass Ginger Dressing

SERVES 4

1 bay leaf

Handful of black peppercorns

1 teaspoon red wine vinegar

1 whole octopus, about 750g–1kg, cleaned (from the fishmonger, or see opposite)

SALAD

150g (1 cup) cherry tomatoes – whole if tiny, or halved

80g (1 cup) shredded green and red baby capsicum (or ordinary large capsicum)

About 200g cucumber, peeled, deseeded and diced (to make about 1 cup)

4–5 spring onions, sliced (to make about ½ cup)

DRESSING

3 lemongrass stalks, roughly chopped

3 tablespoons extra-virgin olive oil

Juice of ½ lime, plus extra, if needed

3cm piece of ginger

Salt and pepper

Fill a large pan with water and bring to the boil. Add the bay leaf, peppercorns and the vinegar then put the octopus into the pot and simmer very gently for about 45 minutes, or until tender.

Let the octopus cool in the cooking liquid and then remove it. Remove the skin, which should slip off quite easily when pulled with your fingers.

Meanwhile, prepare your salad dressing. Put the lemongrass stalks into a mortar and give them a good pounding with the pestle to crush the stems. Add the olive oil. Pound them together a bit more and then leave for 30 minutes or so for the flavours to infuse. Tip the mixture into a sieve over a bowl to strain out the lemongrass (press it in the sieve to extract every last bit of flavour). Discard the lemongrass (or use in a soup or curry).

Add the juice of half a lime to the lemongrass-infused oil.

Grate the ginger, put the pulp in the sieve, then hold it over the dressing and press it to extract the juice. Add some salt and pepper, taste and adjust the seasonings as necessary. You may want more lime juice, salt or pepper.

Put the salad ingredients in a large bowl and combine them gently.

Grill the octopus for about 10 minutes on a barbecue, turning once, until nicely charred. As soon as it's cool enough to handle, cut it into bite-sized chunks then add to the salad vegetables. Pour over the dressing and toss the whole lot gently together. Allow to stand for 10–20 minutes, then toss again, taste and adjust the seasonings if necessary before taking it to the table.

TO PREPARE AN OCTOPUS

If you have caught your own octopus, the easiest method to dispatch it is to turn its whole head inside out. To do this, slide two of your fingers up into the hood on the back of the head, then firmly grip the hood and turn the head inside out. This will kill the octopus instantly. Remove the brain and intestinal matter. If purchasing a whole octopus from the fishmonger, you'll also need to turn the head inside out to remove all the internal organs, taking particular care not to rupture the ink sack.

Give the inside of the head a good rinse. Return the head back to its original position and use a small sharp knife to cut around the eyes and remove them. Pinch the head just above the beak and give it a good squeeze – this will force the beak out so that it can be removed using a knife.

Give the whole octopus a good rinse, and it is ready to cook.

Summer barbecues don't have to be all sausages and onion. Squid loves the barbecue treatment and when coupled with a tangy dressing and fresh salad it makes a worthy addition to any grill lord's repertoire.

Barbecued Squid Salad

SERVES 4

4 whole, medium-sized squid

1 red onion, finely chopped

1 Lebanese cucumber, halved lengthways and sliced

2 mild red chillies, seeds removed, finely chopped

1 avocado, roughly diced

2 handfuls of rocket

Small bunch of coriander, leaves picked

Olive oil, for grilling

Salt and pepper

1 lime

DRESSING

60ml (¼ cup) extra-virgin olive oil

Splash of sherry vinegar (or balsamic or red wine vinegar)

2 garlic cloves, finely chopped

Clean your squid by separating the eyes, beak and tentacles from the hood. Remove any internal organs as well as the quill from inside the hood and give it a good rinse. Cut the eyes away from above the tentacles and pop the beak out. Cut along one side of each of the hoods to open them out into a long, flat piece. Lightly score the inside of each hood in a cross-hatch pattern. If you don't have the time or inclination to clean a whole squid then your fishmonger should be able to provide you with scored pieces.

Combine the onion, cucumber and chilli in a salad bowl. Toss through the avocado, along with the rocket and coriander leaves.

To make the dressing, combine the extra-virgin olive oil, sherry vinegar and garlic.

Heat a barbecue grill so that it's nice and hot. Massage a little olive oil into the squid and then season with salt and pepper. Cook on the grill for long enough to get some nice crusty grill lines – a minute or two on each side will be plenty.

Remove the squid from the grill and thinly slice the hoods and separate the tentacles. Squeeze the lime over the top and toss the squid through the salad. Lightly dress the salad and serve straight away.

On a crisp, sunny afternoon, there are few better ways
to cater for a hungry horde than a big pan of gently
simmering paella. The sight of the saffron-infused rice
studded with tasty morsels of rabbit, seafood and fresh
herbs is a sure-fire way to set mouths watering.

South Coast Paella

SERVES 6

Olive oil, for frying

6 baby leeks, green part
trimmed, halved vertically

6 spring onions, finely sliced
on an angle

50g air-cured, free-range
bacon, rind removed, cut into
batons

1 medium red onion,
finely sliced

4 garlic cloves, chopped

80ml white wine

1 sprig of rosemary, leaves
picked and chopped

1 bay leaf

1 teaspoon smoked paprika

800ml chicken stock (see
page 208)

12 saffron strands, soaked
in the stock overnight

300g Australian short-grain rice

2 confit rabbit legs, meat
shredded (if you don't have
this you could use duck
confit, page 206, or 2 cooked
free-range chicken thighs)

12 fresh mussels

250g flathead tail fillets, cut
into bite-sized chunks

1 small tender, cooked octopus
(or squid), thinly sliced

Generous handful of snow peas,
cut in half

Chopped flat-leaf parsley and
lemon wedges, to serve

Heat a paella pan or large frypan on the stove over a medium-
high heat and add a generous splash of olive oil. Add the baby
leeks and spring onions and cook until slightly browned and
then set aside.

Add the bacon to the pan and fry until it is brown and crispy,
then add the red onion and sauté until soft, then add the garlic.
Pour in the wine, add the rosemary, bay leaf and paprika, and
bring it to the boil. Pour in the stock with the saffron, then bring
it to the boil once more.

Pour the rice into the pan, stirring to distribute the ingredients.
Sprinkle the shredded rabbit over the top of the paella and reduce
the heat to low. From now on, don't stir the paella – this helps a
delicious crust of rice, known as the socarrat, form on the bottom
of the pan. Watch that it doesn't burn, though.

Once the rice has absorbed half the stock, push the mussels,
flathead pieces, octopus and snow peas into the simmering liquid.

When the stock has all but disappeared (just a little bubbling
through the rice), check the rice to make sure it's cooked. If it's
done, turn off the heat and leave the paella to settle for
5 minutes before serving.

Garnish with parsley, the leeks and spring onions and lemon
wedges, then serve straight from the pan, making sure that
everyone gets a piece of the crusty rice from the bottom of
the pan.

Wild blue mussels are found in many of the temperate
waterways around southern Australia. Their plump,
juicy flesh is a real treat when freshly steamed open
and eaten, unadulterated, straight from the shell.
If you're after something a little more complex on the
flavour front then a light smoke is the perfect partner
to the salty sweetness of the mussel. Smoking is a
simple process and something that people have been
doing for centuries – if you've never tried it, here's a
great place to start.

Smoked Blue Mussels

SERVES 4

1.5kg blue mussels

First, make sure you have a wok with a tight-fitting lid, and a
rack that can sit inside it. You'll also need a small handful of
wood shavings – I prefer Black Wattle but any commercially
bought smoking chip will do, though they are mostly imported.
Other home-grown options include dried banksia pods and
Mountain Ash sawdust.

Clean the mussels by removing their beards (sorry, boys!) and
giving them a quick scrub to remove any grit or growths on the
outside of the shell. Place them in a pot filled with 1cm of water
and heat until it starts to boil, then simmer with the lid on until
they have all just begun to open. Take the mussels out of their
shells, discard the shells and put the mussels to one side while
you prepare the wok for smoking.

Make a vessel for your smoking chips by folding a 30cm piece
of foil in half and rolling each edge in a little towards the centre.
Put it in the bottom of the wok. Place the smoking chips on top
and heat the wok until the chips begin to gently smoulder. Put
the rack in the wok and place the mussel flesh on top. Cover the
wok and smoke for around 10 minutes or until the smoke has
imparted its subtle flavour to the mussels.

You can eat the mussels straight from the wok or if you want
to do a big batch and save some for later you can transfer
the mussels to a sterilised jar (see page 23) and cover with a
neutral-flavoured oil, such as rice bran oil. Keep them in the
fridge and eat them within the month.

The area around where I live is known as Australia's oyster coast due to the abundance of pristine estuaries that produce some of the nation's finest oysters. This is particularly fortuitous for me, as I can eat natural oysters 'til the cows come home. However, every now and then, especially in the cooler months, I like to make something a little heartier and that's where the oyster pie comes in. Nothing overly complicated: just a rich, creamy oyster filling and a flaky, buttery, rough puff pastry top. If you don't have time to make the pastry fear not – a couple of sheets of store-bought, frozen puff pastry will also do the job.

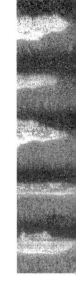

Oyster Pot Pie

SERVES 2

ROUGH PUFF PASTRY

250g (1⅔ cups) plain flour, plus extra for dusting

Salt

250g cold butter, cut into walnut-sized cubes

Ice-cold water

1 free-range egg, lightly beaten, for glazing

OYSTER FILLING

3 dozen oysters, still on the shell

Oil, for frying

½ brown onion, finely diced

1 celery stick, finely diced

1 spring onion, finely diced

1 garlic clove, finely chopped

½ mild red chilli, seeds removed, finely sliced

Salt and pepper

1 teaspoon cornflour

50ml (¼ cup) double cream

A squeeze of lemon juice

Small bunch of flat-leaf parsley leaves, finely chopped

To make the pastry, sift the plain flour into a mixing bowl and add a pinch of salt. Toss the butter in the flour until coated. The butter must be cold if the finished pastry is to be crisp and flaky (rather than greasy). Add a little ice-cold water and use your hands to bring the dough together. The dough will have walnut-sized lumps but don't stress because that is exactly what it should have.

Lightly flour your kitchen bench and turn the dough out onto it. Roughly shape the dough into a rectangle and roll it out until it's about 2cm thick. Fold the dough into thirds using what's called a book fold. It sounds tricky but all you have to do is take the two edges and fold them one-third of the way into the centre so that they overlap, as though you're folding up a pamphlet. Rotate the dough 90 degrees and repeat the process of rolling, folding and rotating the dough. If the pastry starts to get a little soft, let it rest folded and uncovered in the fridge for half an hour, then take it out and start again. Four or five turns should do the trick – by this stage the butter should be well incorporated into the pastry. Fold the pastry one last time and rest in the fridge for an hour before rolling it out. If you're feeling particularly motivated you can double the recipe and split the pastry into two after the final turn. Rest one for use straight away and wrap the other in cling film and store in the freezer for later.

Now you can make the filling while the pastry is resting.

Shuck the oysters and reserve the liquid. If you aren't a confident shucker you can steam them lightly in a pan on a low heat (with the lid on) and reserve the liquor. Don't wash the oysters or you'll wash away the flavour. If there are bits of shell on them, gently brush the shell away and strain the liquid through a fine sieve to catch any bits of grit, shell or sand.

Using a deep-sided frypan on a medium heat, fry the diced onion and celery in a little oil until they are soft. Add the spring onion, garlic, chilli and season with salt. Add the cornflour and gently stir and cook – the cornflour will help make the pie filling thick without affecting the flavour. Add the oyster liquor, cream and lemon juice, stirring constantly until the mixture thickens. Next add the oysters and cook just until the oysters start to curl, about 2 minutes. Season to taste. Remove the oyster mixture from the heat, add the parsley, and let it cool to room temperature.

Preheat your oven to 190°C. Lightly grease 2 x 13cm oval pie tins or 1 x 25cm round pie tin.

Once your filling is cool, pour it into your pie dishes. Roll the dough out on a floured work surface to a thickness of 3mm and cut rounds to fit over the top of the pie dishes, allowing for a slight overhang. Place the pastry over the filled pies and press the edges to seal. Cut slits in the top of each pie to allow steam to escape and brush with egg wash. Transfer to a baking tray and bake until the crust is golden – about 35 minutes. Allow to cool slightly before serving.

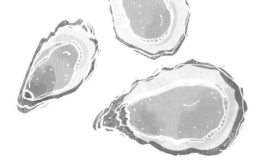

Sea Urchin on Toast

SERVES 4

12 sea urchins

Lightly flavoured olive oil

A few sprigs of flat-leaf parsley, finely chopped

Zest and juice of 1 lemon

4 slices crusty bread

Cultured butter (see page 240)

Salt

To prepare the sea urchins you need a glove to protect your hand from the quills, a pair of kitchen shears, a spoon and a sink to work in. Use the shears to cut a hole around the mouth that's a bit bigger than a 50 cent coin. Pour out the liquid and discard any black bits, which are partially digested food. The roe, best in winter and spring, are what you want: these are the orange parts – use a spoon to scoop them out. Rinse the roe under cold water, gently shake dry and then place in a bowl.

Drizzle the olive oil over the roe, add a good pinch of finely chopped parsley and the lemon zest. Leave that to sit while you toast your bread.

Generously slather the toast with butter and then top with the urchin roe. Drizzle the lemon juice over the top and finish with the tiniest sprinkle of salt.

MEAT

I have a long-standing love affair with meat. Like a lot of folk of my parents' vintage, my Mum was a cook of the meat-with-every-meal variety, while the only time Dad would cook was on Sundays – bacon and eggs for breakfast, barbecues for lunch. I loved it all – the roasts, the half-burnt snags, the bacon, the stews. I couldn't get enough. Veggies were nothing but an unnecessary distraction – something to feed to the dog under the table. Not only was I an enthusiastic consumer, I also considered myself to be quite well informed because even as a kid I knew that beef came from cows, bacon came from pigs and chicken came from, well, chickens. What I didn't realise until much later in life was that there's much more to being a carnivore than meets the eye.

When I first moved to the farm at Tilba, the thing that I was most excited about was having the opportunity to try my hand at raising my own meat. For most of my life, meat had been something that was purchased from the supermarket or the butcher. Thinking of myself as a responsible consumer, I always tried to purchase the most ethically raised meat that I could afford. I sought out meat that was free range, pasture fed, free of antibiotics and hormones. Despite the sense of comfort that these words offered me, I couldn't help but feel a level of disconnect. I ate meat almost every day but I had absolutely no part in producing it. Now that I was on the farm, I finally had the chance to take total responsibility for raising my own meat and everything that entailed.

With absolutely no experience in rearing livestock, the learning curve was steep. The pigs needed to be fed like clockwork. They'd constantly knock over their water to make a wallow and on more than one occasion they escaped their enclosure to have a root around in the veggie patch. My cattle would instinctively find any weak spots in my boundary fence and then squeeze through to go and have a frolic with the neighbour's herd. My meat chickens had to be moved at least once a day, fed twice a day and were constantly under threat from all manner of remorseless predators. I quickly realised that these animals were totally dependent on me for their wellbeing. I fed them, I supplied them with water and I made

sure that they were happy and free from harm. These daily rituals of livestock husbandry were having an unexpected side effect. I was beginning to grow very fond of the livestock under my care. They would recognise me – and the ever-present feed bucket – and grunt, moo or cheep with excitement. I knew their individual faces and behaviour; it was beautiful. Though all the while, right in the back of my mind I knew that I would be personally responsible not just for their lives, but their deaths as well.

Nothing could have prepared me mentally for sending my first beast to slaughter. On the one hand I was excited about the prospect of finally having the chance to try my own farm-reared meat. On the other hand, the thought of being responsible for ending a life just so I could eat was weighing heavily on my mind. Prior to this, I could always walk into a butcher and order great armfuls of meat and not give a second thought to the fact that all those cuts were once part of a living, breathing animal. All that nasty business was happening behind closed doors, in an abattoir far, far away. Out of sight, out of mind.

Back on the farm there was no escaping the reality that was about to unfold for my first farm-reared pig. With the expert assistance of the local slaughterman, I calmly corralled the young boar into a little pen, gave him a bit of feed as a distraction and then watched as his life was instantly ended with a deftly placed bullet behind the ear. There was no time to reflect on what had just unfolded; time was of the essence and the fresh carcass had to be bled and eviscerated, and the hair removed. We worked quickly and silently until a clean pink carcass was hung on the butcher's hook. Now my prize pig didn't look any different to the hundreds of others that I had seen out the back of butchers' shops over the years. The only difference was that I knew exactly how much work went into getting to this point. I vowed to appreciate every mouthful of that animal and not to waste a skerrick.

As you'd expect, the meat from that first pig was far better than any other pork I had ever tasted. It wasn't just the deliciously marbled, ruby-coloured flesh, the delicately flavoured offal or the incomparably crispy crackling. There was another dimension to the taste, one that can't be described using the five classic elements of taste. Every single mouthful filled me with a sense of satisfaction because I knew that I had been personally responsible for the life and welfare of the animal that I was eating, and judging by the flavour, I'd done a stand-up job.

I realise that it's not possible for everyone to raise their own meat but I feel that as meat-eaters we need to know where our meat comes from. Not everyone can live on an 8-hectare farm and spend all day looking after animals but that definitely does not excuse us from caring about the systems that are used to rear our meat and the welfare of the animals in those systems.

Australians eat an enormous amount of meat. It's estimated that each of us gobbles up an incredible 111kg of the stuff every year. Multiply that over the entire population and you start to get an idea of just how big a business meat is. To satisfy that demand, sectors of the agricultural community have turned to industrial methods in order to maximise output. On paper this makes perfect sense; less land is required, inputs are closely monitored and output is increased. Raising livestock becomes an exercise in accounting rather than animal husbandry.

Unfortunately it's not as simple as that. Intensive industrial systems may provide us with a bounty of cheap meat, but that low price at the checkout doesn't take into account the social, environmental and long-term economic impacts of production. Intensive livestock-raising practices work against nature and are responsible for agricultural land degradation, air and water pollution, loss of habitat and biodiversity and excessive use of hormones, chemicals and antibiotics. On top of that, the meat is flavourless, watery and nutritionally deficient. Why on earth, then, is this inferior meat still being produced? Because we're asking for it. If all we care about as meat consumers is price and availability then we have no one to blame for the rubbish that we consume but ourselves.

It's not all doom and gloom, though. As consumers we have an incredible amount of power to influence the way that our meat is produced. It's time that we stopped stumbling blindly into supermarkets and grabbing the cheapest things off the shelves. We need to start asking serious questions about the quality of meat that we consume. Have the livestock that we eat been allowed to express their natural instincts? Have they had access to adequate pasture and sunshine? Are they naturally healthy or do they need a cocktail of antibiotics to survive? Start asking these questions wherever you get your meat; if no one can answer your questions, then find somewhere where they can. There are loads of quality meat producers out there who genuinely care about the welfare of their animals and the sustainability of their farms. The more people who seek out ethically and sustainably produced meat,

the more farmers will turn to these production systems. We need to adapt a meat-eating culture of quality over quantity.

I've chosen the recipes in this chapter to use a wide range of cuts and offal, not just the cuts traditionally considered to be prime cuts. If an animal has been well raised then there should be no such thing as a secondary cut; every cut should be thought of as being of premium quality. All it takes to get the most out of a cut of meat is a little knowledge, a bit of technique and a lot of love. These recipes are about celebrating the best that meat has to offer us and it all begins with quality ingredients. So whether you raise your own or you buy it from someone else, take a moment to consider what goes into putting meat on the table. For better or worse, our choices as meat consumers have consequences that reach far beyond our own kitchens.

If you don't know how to prepare a beautiful roast chicken I suggest you make that the very next thing to master on your cooking odyssey. A well-roasted bird is the gift that keeps on giving: not only do you get to enjoy it for dinner, there's usually plenty of meat left over for a salad or a sanga the next day and then, after all the meat is gone, you can use the carcass for a stock.

Perfect Roast Chicken

SERVES 6

1 free-range chicken (around 1.8kg is a good size for a family)

Oil, for frying

1 large brown onion, cut in half vertically, skin on

Salt and pepper

Small bunch of thyme

Knob of butter, softened

Remove the chicken from the fridge an hour before you intend to cook it.

Preheat the oven to 200°C and place your roasting tray in the oven.

Heat a little oil in a frypan over a medium heat, add the onion cut-side down, and fry until the bottom is nicely browned. Remove the two halves from the pan and put to one side.

Generously season the bird both inside and out. If your knife skills are up to it, remove the wishbone. This isn't essential but it does making carving a lot easier later. Stuff the caramelised onion halves into the cavity with half the thyme. Gently separate the skin from the breast meat by working a couple of fingers between them, starting at the neck cavity and pushing up towards the drumsticks. When the skin is loose, massage the softened butter and a few sprigs of thyme into the breast meat.

Then, a simple way to truss the chicken is to take both of the wings and tuck the tips under the body. Next, make an incision in the skin just below the knuckle of one drumstick, so that the knuckle of the other drumstick can be tucked over the first and through the incision. This tucked-up, cannonball shape will help your bird cook evenly. If you buy a chicken and the skin has been cut off below the knuckle, you can truss it by tying it with string.

Put the chicken on the hot tray and roast it at 200°C for 15 minutes, until the skin is starting to brown. Now turn the oven down to 160°C and cook for an hour. Turning the temperature down like this will allow the bird to cook gently without drying out.

To check if your bird is ready insert the tip of a knife into the deepest part of the thigh joint. If a little blood comes out, pop it back in the oven for a while. If the liquid is clear then you are good to go.

Remove from the oven, cover in foil, and rest for at least 15 minutes. This allows the juices to evenly distribute back through the flesh.

Carve and serve with lashings of homemade gravy (see page 146). Don't throw out those onions either – they make a great side for your roast.

The crowning jewel to any roast dinner is a rich, velvety gravy, made from flavour-packed roasting juices, a touch of flour and a little homemade stock. It takes a *bit* more effort than mixing up the packet stuff but your efforts are doubly rewarded by superb taste and the adulation of your dinner guests.

Gravy

MAKES ENOUGH TO
ACCOMPANY A ROAST

A roasting tray of juices from a joint of meat that has just come out of the oven

1 tablespoon plain flour

500ml (2 cups) stock (chicken stock for lighter meats, beef stock for red meats – see pages 208 and 209)

Salt and pepper

When your joint of meat has finished roasting, take it out of the tray and set it aside some place warm to rest while you make the gravy.

Pour or spoon most of the excess fat off the juices left in the roasting tray, leaving a little fat behind or adding some duck fat (see page 205) to enrich the flavour of your gravy.

Place the roasting tray over a medium heat and sprinkle in the flour, then use a wooden spoon to scrape up any crispy bits on the bottom of the tray and mix the juices and flour together. Cook for a couple of minutes, being careful not to let it stick and burn. Pour in half the stock and stir to combine, then add the rest of the stock and gradually reduce to the desired consistency.

Season with salt and pepper and serve.

When it comes to roasting chickens, not all birds are created equal, and not every bird that comes through the kitchen is young, plump and juicy. Older birds tend to be a little stringier and a little drier but, luckily, what they lack in these departments they more than make up for in the flavour stakes. Using a salt-pastry shell seals in all the juices and gently steams the bird, resulting in moist, tender meat. Adding a little thyme, garlic and wine to the pastry shell enhances the flavour even further.

Chicken in a Garlic Salt Crust

SERVES 4

600g (4 cups) plain flour

600g (2 cups) salt

250ml (1 cup) white wine

1 head of garlic, cloves peeled

1 medium free-range chicken

Small bunch of thyme

Olive oil

In a big mixing bowl combine the flour with the salt. Steadily pour in the wine, using your hand to mix until a dough forms.

Turn the dough out onto a lightly floured bench and knead it until it becomes smooth and pliable, then set it aside.

Thinly slice half the garlic cloves and lightly smash the other half. Stuff the smashed cloves into the cavity of the chicken with half the thyme sprigs.

Preheat the oven to 180°C.

Roll out the dough to about 1cm thick, and large enough to wrap around the bird. Scatter the pastry with the sliced garlic and the picked leaves of the remaining thyme. Place the chicken in the centre of the dough, breast side down. Wrap the pastry up around the bird, pressing around the joints to get rid of any air pockets. Tuck in the pastry, then turn the bird around so the smooth side is facing up. Patch any holes in the pastry to create an airtight wrap for the bird.

Lightly drizzle a baking dish with olive oil and place the wrapped chicken inside. Bake in the oven for 1 hour, until the dough is like a firm crust and the internal temperature of the chicken has reached 75°C. You can measure this by pushing a kitchen thermometer through the crust into the thigh meat. If you don't have a kitchen thermometer, then push a long thin knife into the thigh meat. Leave it for 30 seconds, then pull it out and carefully touch the tip of the knife to the skin on the inside of your wrist. If it is too hot to leave in place, then the chicken is good to go.

For maximum impact on your fellow diners break open the crust at the table and carve the steaming, aromatic chicken. You can't eat the crust but it sure makes for a grand entrance.

Living in a regional area and being a poultry enthusiast, I take great pleasure in being able to keep a big, handsome rooster with my laying hens. My little rural idyll wouldn't be complete without his confident crow, even if he does feel the need to let it rip at five in the morning. The girls don't really need him but they do seem to enjoy the company and the tasty morsels that he selflessly digs up and shares.

Having a rooster also allows me to breed my own stock but while the young pullets make welcome additions to my laying flock, you only need so many rooster alarm clocks going off first thing in the morning. What to do with surplus cockerels and roosters, with their pronounced taste and often stringy flesh, is an old question, one that is perfectly answered by a salty and sumptuous braise in red wine. If you don't have a rooster you could just substitute a regular chook.

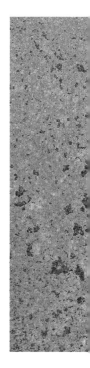

Coq au Vin

SERVES **4**

Oil, for frying

250g bacon (see page 193), cut into batons

2 carrots, roughly diced

2 brown onions, roughly diced

4 garlic cloves, minced

**1 rooster, jointed
(2 drumsticks, 2 thighs,
2 breasts)**

2 tablespoons plain flour, seasoned

60ml (¼ cup) cognac

750ml (1 bottle) red wine

Rooster giblets (liver, heart, feet)

3 bay leaves

A few sprigs of thyme

GARNISH

250g button mushrooms

Oil, for frying

2 big knobs of butter, for frying

Place a deep-sided frypan over a medium heat, add a little oil, then fry the bacon batons until browned. Remove from the pan and set aside. Add the carrot and onion and continue cooking until they have softened and started to colour, then add the garlic and cook until soft and aromatic. Transfer the contents to a bowl with the bacon.

Lightly dust the rooster pieces (not the giblets) in the seasoned flour, return the pan to the heat and fry the rooster until brown all over.

Add the cognac and the wine, using a wooden spoon to scrape any tasty, crusty bits from the bottom of the pan.

Add the fried bacon and veggies, the giblets, the bay leaves and the thyme to the pan. If the rooster isn't completely covered in liquid, top up with a little wine, chicken stock or water. Bring the pan to the boil, then lower the heat and simmer uncovered for an hour or until the meat comes easily away from the bone.

While the rooster is cooking, make the garnish.

To start, wipe the mushrooms and cut any larger ones into bite-sized pieces. Place a pan over a medium–high heat and add a splash of cooking oil and a knob of butter. When the butter starts to foam, toss in the mushrooms, season with salt and loads of pepper and fry until browned. Remove from the heat and keep warm.

Salt and pepper

10 small white cocktail onions, peeled

6 slices white bread, trimmed, halved diagonally

Small handful of flat-leaf parsley, chopped

In a small saucepan, melt the remaining knob of butter over a very low heat, then add a little salt and pepper and the cocktail onions, put on the lid and cook for 20–30 minutes. They are done when soft and caramelised. Reserve the onion butter.

To make the croutons, heat some butter over a low heat, add the onion butter and fry the bread until golden and crisp.

To serve, arrange the rooster pieces on a platter with the croutons on the side. Garnish with the onions, mushrooms and fresh parsley. Accompany with a big bowl of steamed potatoes or a bowl of creamy polenta.

This spicy North African–style marinade adds a chilli kick to grilled chicken, as well as a sweet, smoky flavour. Served with a simple scoop of couscous and a dollop of fire-quelling yoghurt, chicken off the grill never tasted so good. Your local butcher will butterfly the chicken if you ask them nicely.

Butterflied Chicken with Harissa

SERVES 4

Handful of medium-heat red chillies (such as Serrano), tops removed

4 garlic cloves, peeled

3 teaspoons cumin seeds, toasted

1 teaspoon coriander seeds, toasted

1 teaspoon ground smoked paprika

Handful of cherry tomatoes

60ml (¼ cup) olive oil

Zest and juice of 1 lemon

Salt

1 medium free-range, pasture-fed chicken, butterflied

200g couscous

200ml chicken stock (see page 208), boiling hot

Knob of butter

Salt and pepper

200ml natural yoghurt (see page 245)

Extra-virgin olive oil

Small handful each of mint and coriander leaves, roughly torn

Lemon wedges, to serve

Put the chillies, garlic, cumin and coriander seeds, paprika and cherry tomatoes in a food processor. Pulse until a paste starts to form. Add the olive oil, half the lemon juice and zest and a generous pinch of salt and pulse again until combined but not completely smooth. If you don't have a food processor you can smash everything together in a large mortar and pestle.

Lay the chicken out in a deep-sided dish and season with salt. Coat with the harissa marinade and rub it all over. If you have the time, place in the fridge to marinate for a couple of hours.

Heat the chargrill plate of the barbecue over a medium–high heat and place the chicken on, skin-side down. Cook until the skin is charred and then turn over and repeat for the other side. If the skin is charring and the flesh still isn't cooked, move the chicken to a cooler part of the plate and grill for around 15–20 minutes, turning occasionally, until it's cooked through.

Meanwhile, place the couscous in a heat-proof bowl, pour over the hot chicken stock, cover and allow to stand for 10 minutes. Then toss in a knob of butter, season with salt and pepper and fluff with a fork.

To make the yoghurt dressing, combine the yoghurt, remaining lemon zest and juice and a large pinch of salt in a small bowl, then stir to combine. Drizzle over a little extra-virgin olive oil and stir through. Scatter with some of the mint leaves.

To serve, place couscous on a large plate and top with the grilled chicken. Scatter over the rest of the mint and the coriander leaves and serve with the yoghurt dressing and lemon wedges on the side.

Chicken wings make one of the best barbecued snacks – they're small enough to manage without the need for a plate and there's lots of juicy morsels of meat wrapped up among the easily navigated bones. I like to marinate my wings in a sweet, hoppy, citrusy marinade overnight to give them an extra lift before their date with the hotplate.

Beer-marinated Chicken Wings

SERVES 6 AS A SNACK

3 garlic cloves, finely chopped

2 tablespoons rice bran oil

750ml (3 cups) hoppy beer, such as a pale ale

Zest and juice of 2 limes

3 tablespoons honey

1kg free-range, pasture-fed chicken wings

Salt and pepper

2 tablespoons dried chilli flakes

2 large sprigs rosemary, leaves picked

2 tablespoons salt flakes

Lime wedges, to serve

In a large bowl, mix together the garlic, oil, beer, lime zest and juice and honey. Toss through the chicken wings, season well with salt and pepper and marinate in the refrigerator overnight.

Preheat a barbecue grill so that it's nice and hot.

Remove the wings from the marinade and place them straight onto the grill for 10–15 minutes. Brush over any of the excess marinade as the wings cook.

Meanwhile, in a mortar and pestle, grind the chilli flakes and rosemary leaves, then add the salt flakes and grind again to combine the three ingredients.

Serve the wings on a big plate with a couple of wedges of lime and a generous sprinkle of the chilli and rosemary salt.

When you kill your own chickens you have access to lots of different offal and offcuts that don't usually pop up on your local supermarket shelf. Chicken feet are a prime example. A tray of barbecued chicken feet, packed with flavour and lip-smacking gelatine, is sure to raise a few eyebrows – but adventurous eaters will be rewarded with morsels of sticky skin, tasty meat and a bone to gnaw on.

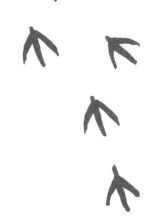

Barbecued Chicken Feet

SERVES 4 AS A SNACK

1kg chicken feet

2 tablespoons rice bran oil

250ml (1 cup) Chinese rice wine vinegar

250ml (1 cup) soy sauce

1 teaspoon sesame oil

3 star anise

2 cinnamon sticks

2 teaspoons dried chilli flakes

6 garlic cloves, sliced

100g (½ cup) brown sugar

Salt flakes and dried chilli flakes, to serve

Wash the chicken feet in a large bowl of salted water and remove the scaly outer skin (if you're lucky, your butcher has already done this for you).

Place the feet in a saucepan of simmering, salted water and cook for 10 minutes, removing any scum that comes to the surface. Strain the feet in a colander and let stand until cool enough to handle.

Put the feet on a wooden board and use a sharp knife to trim the nails and then discard.

Transfer the feet to a deep-sided, heavy-based frypan and add the remaining ingredients. Cook over a medium heat, turning the feet occasionally, until the sauce is sticky, caramelised and reduced.

Preheat a grill or barbecue until hot. Chargrill the feet, then serve as an appetiser or snack accompanied by a small bowl of salt and chilli flakes.

If the legs of a duck are perfect for a confit then the breasts are at their best when panfried, crispy-skinned and pink in the middle. Duck breasts have a thick layer of fat under the skin that renders during cooking, a little like a built-in baster, leaving the meat moist and full of fabulous flavour.

Crispy-skinned Duck Breasts

SERVES 4

4 free-range Muscovy duck breasts

Salt flakes and pepper

Bring the duck breasts to room temperature and using a sharp knife score the skin in a crosshatch pattern, being careful to only score the skin and fat and not cut the flesh. Season generously with salt and pepper.

Place a heavy-based frypan over a medium heat.

When the pan is hot place the duck breasts, skin-side down, in the pan. Cook until most of the fat under the skin has rendered out and the skin is crispy and golden – about 6 minutes.

Turn the duck breasts over and cook for another 2–3 minutes, spooning over the rendered fat. It's best to serve the breasts so that they are pink in the middle for maximum moisture and flavour. When cooked the breast should have firmed slightly but still be pink in the centre.

Transfer to a board and leave to rest for 5 minutes.

To serve, slice the breasts and accompany with a sweet, port-based sauce, some crunchy, blanched greens and a big spoonful of mashed potato.

We've all been there. We've all parted the plastic curtains of a local takeaway shop to be greeted by a bain-marie full of golden, fried treats. We know it's probably been sitting there for the last 12 hours, we know that it was made in a factory somewhere and that we'll feel like rubbish after we eat it but we go ahead and order one anyway. I often imagine the culinary minds who devised such deep-fried delicacies. Surely the prototypes were made in home kitchens, using fresh ingredients. So I decided to try making my own version of the most iconic of the bain-marie battlers, the chiko roll, using a simple egg pastry and a veggie-rich, meaty filling. Here's my tribute to this Aussie classic.

Cheeky Rolls

MAKES 8

220g (1 cup) barley

2 medium zucchini, halved, deseeded, cut into fine strips

1 x 1kg lamb leg, deboned, trimmed of fat and cut into 4cm chunks (or use high-quality lamb mince)

Oil, for frying

½ teaspoon celery seeds

2 carrots, finely sliced

2 medium brown onions, halved and finely sliced

Handful of green beans, finely sliced

2 celery sticks, finely sliced

Salt and pepper

1 free-range egg, lightly beaten

500ml (2 cups) rice bran oil (or similar), for deep-frying

EGG PASTRY

600g (4 cups) plain flour

4 free-range eggs

1 teaspoon salt

250ml (1 cup) iced water

Begin by making the egg pastry. Pile the flour onto a clean, dry bench and make a well in the centre. Crack in the eggs and sprinkle over a pinch of salt. Using a fork, lightly beat the eggs without drawing in any flour. Add a little of the water and lightly beat. Now you can gradually start to bring in the flour. Slowly add the remaining water and then work everything together with your hands to form a dough. Knead for around 5 minutes or until the dough is smooth. Shape the dough into a disc, wrap it up in some cling film and let it rest in the fridge for half an hour.

Now you can start the filling. Pour the barley into a pot along with 750ml water and a pinch of salt. Bring the pot up to a simmer and let it bubble away for around half an hour. The barley is cooked when it is soft but with a little resistance. Drain and rinse the grains with cold water.

Put the zucchini strips into a colander set over a bowl and lightly sprinkle with salt to help draw out any excess moisture. After 15 minutes squeeze out any water and pat the zucchini dry.

Using a hand-cranked mincer, mince the lamb and season well with salt and pepper. If you don't have a mincer then use high-quality lamb mince from your local butcher.

Heat a little oil in a frypan over a high heat, add the mince and celery seeds and fry for about 5 minutes, or until the meat is nice and brown. Remove the mince from the pan and set aside.

Add a little more oil to the same pan, turn the heat to medium and add the carrots, onion, beans and celery. Sauté the vegetables for about 5 minutes until they have softened. Add the drained zucchini and continue frying until it is soft and cooked. Season with salt and pepper and remove from the heat.

Combine the cooked mince, barley and fried vegetables in a large bowl, check the seasoning, then place in the fridge to cool.

Cut the pastry in half and roll out one piece on a lightly floured bench until it's 2–3mm thick and about 25cm x 15cm in size. Cut into four evenly sized rectangles. Take one of the rectangles, and with the long edge facing you spoon 3 tablespoons of the chilled mixture along it. Leave a 2cm gap between the filling and the edge of the pastry at either side.

Lightly brush the edges of the pastry rectangle with the beaten egg. Fold the short edges over the mixture at both ends, then fold the long edge over the mixture and roll up to form a thick, large spring roll shape. Place on a sheet of baking paper and set aside. Repeat until all the pastry and filling has been used. Place in the fridge for half an hour before cooking.

While the rolls are resting, heat the rice bran oil in a large, heavy-based saucepan until it reaches 170°C. To test if the oil is hot enough, throw in a small piece of bread – it should turn golden in 20–25 seconds. Cook the rolls in batches of two or three, so the oil stays hot. Cook the rolls for around 5 minutes, turning them regularly, until the pastry is golden and cooked through. Transfer to a paper towel to drain and eat while still hot.

Wild rabbit responds incredibly well to cooking twice because it is such a lean and gamey meat. Farmed rabbit could be substituted for wild, but there are very few free-range rabbit farmers around and the politics of rabbit farming are very similar to those of the chicken industry. If you do use farmed rabbits, remember they are generally fattier and have softer meat texture, which means that they will need a shorter braising time.

Wild Rabbit, Braised and Fried

SERVES 4

2 whole wild rabbits, skinned, gutted, jointed

Salt and pepper

Olive oil

A sprig of sage

2 heads of garlic, cut in half horizontally

375ml (½ bottle) white wine

500ml (2 cups) chicken stock (see page 208), veggie stock (see page 59) or water

1 litre (4 cups) rice bran oil (or similar), for deep-frying

Salt flakes and lemon wedges, to serve

CRUMB MIX

75g (½ cup) plain flour, seasoned

4 free-range eggs

125ml (½ cup) full cream milk

200g (2 cups) breadcrumbs

100g (1 cup) Parmesan, finely grated

Take the legs and other joints of the rabbits and pat them dry. Season the rabbit with salt and pepper.

Lay the rabbits in a large saucepan – they should fit snugly. Throw in a glug of olive oil then add the sage and garlic and cover with the wine and the stock. Top up with a little water if necessary – you want all of the pieces covered. Do not brown the rabbit first.

Cover the pan and simmer very gently until the meat is tender and just falling away from the bone. The rabbit should be done after 90 minutes or so (check it from time to time and add more liquid if needed. The length of time of the braise will depend on how long the rabbit has been hung and the age of the animal).

When the rabbit is done take it out of the stock. (The stock isn't needed for this dish, but you don't have to throw it away – it can be used in the same way you would use well-flavoured chicken stock.) Wait until the rabbit is cool enough to handle and pat dry.

For your crumb mix you'll need three bowls. In one bowl put the seasoned flour; in the second whisk the eggs with the milk; and in the third, put the breadcrumbs mixed with half the Parmesan.

Toss the rabbit in flour, then in the egg mix and then roll in the breadcrumb/Parmesan mix. Put the crumbed rabbit pieces on a platter and sprinkle over the remaining Parmesan.

Place a large, heavy-based saucepan on the stove, and heat the oil to 170°C. To test if the oil is hot enough, throw in a small piece of bread – it should turn golden in 20–25 seconds. Add the rabbit pieces a couple at a time, cooking them for around 5 minutes or until golden brown. Take them out and drain well on paper towel.

Sprinkle salt over the rabbit and serve with lemon wedges.

Kangaroo stew, in some form or another, has been bubbling away in pots and camp ovens in this country for more than two hundred years. Before that, kangaroo tail has been slowly cooked under the embers of a campfire all the way back to the Dreamtime. It's only in more recent times that this sustaining dish has dropped from the culinary consciousness.

If you have the appropriate permits you can source your own kangaroo from the wild. Alternatively, seek out a butcher who stocks quality game meat. The tail is generally purchased whole and, when slowly braised on the bone, makes for a flavoursome, lip-smacking meal.

Kanga-ragout

SERVES 4

1 kangaroo tail, cut into
5cm pieces

1 brown onion, roughly diced

2 carrots, roughly diced

1 head of garlic, cloves peeled
and chopped

2 bay leaves

Small bunch of thyme

½ teaspoon black peppercorns

750ml (1 bottle) red wine

Oil, for frying

Salt and pepper

Beef stock (see page 209),
if needed

Small handful of parsley leaves,
roughly chopped

Put the kangaroo pieces into a large mixing bowl with the chopped onion, carrots and garlic. Add the bay leaves, thyme and peppercorns and pour over the red wine. Pop the bowl into the fridge and leave it overnight to marinate. (You can skip this step but the finished dish really does benefit from the little sleep-over in the fridge.)

The next day, remove the roo tail from the marinade and pat the pieces dry. Set the marinade aside.

Heat a deep-sided frypan with a little cooking oil over a medium–high heat.

Season the tail pieces with a little salt and pepper, brown them all over in the pan and then set aside.

Remove the veggies and herbs from the marinade, give them a little shake in a strainer, then fry them in the pan for 2–3 minutes. Place the meat back in the pan, then add the reserved marinade. There should be enough to cover the meat, but if you're a little short, add a touch more wine or some beef stock. (Personally I would steer clear of the beef stock – this dish is all about the roo and using beef stock feels like cheating.)

Bring the wine to a simmer and pop a lid on the pan. Leave that gently bubbling away for at least 2 hours. You'll know it's ready when the meat slides off the bone.

Garnish with parsley and serve with homemade damper (see page 228) or, if you're in the comfort of your home and a long way from the crackle of a campfire, with a large bowl of creamy polenta.

The prime eating cut of a kangaroo is without doubt the loin. Lean, tender and chock full of flavour, it's at its best eaten rare. About an hour before cooking, take the loin out of the fridge and let it come to room temperature — this will avoid any patches of fridge chill on the rare-cooked meat. The robust flavour of kangaroo lends itself perfectly to the earthy sweetness of the beetroot, the hazelnuts add a bit of crunch and the mustard greens cut through the dish with a peppery kick.

Kangaroo with Beetroot and Mustard Greens

SERVES 4

About 8 baby beetroot, stalks trimmed, but tender leaves saved

Oil, for frying

Salt and pepper

1 x 500g kangaroo loin, at room temperature, sinew trimmed

Extra-virgin olive oil

250ml (1 cup) natural yoghurt (see page 245)

Handful of hazelnuts, toasted and roughly chopped

Small bunch of mustard greens

Pop a pot of cold water on the stove, add the beetroots (but not their leaves) and a decent pinch of salt and gently heat to a simmer. Cook for around 20 minutes or until the beetroots are tender when pierced with a knife. Remove the beetroots from the water and leave until cool enough to handle.

Put a frypan on the stove over a medium–high heat, and add a little oil. Season the loin with salt and pepper and then fry for just 2 minutes each side. If you like your meat a little less rare then cook it for an extra minute on each side – just bear in mind that this is one cut of meat that you won't want to be eating well done.

While the kangaroo is resting for a couple of minutes peel the beetroots and cut them into halves from top to bottom.

To serve, slice the kangaroo into 5mm thick slices and arrange on four plates with the beetroots. Drizzle over a little extra-virgin olive oil, spoon on the yoghurt and finish by scattering over the hazelnuts, mustard greens and tender beetroot leaves.

Venison is a flavoursome, lean meat and in this recipe
I've coupled it with native pepperberries, sweet-and-
sour pickled cherries and some creamy labne. As with
all wild proteins, venison barely carries a lick of fat
on it, so I recommend cooking the loin as rare as you
can handle.

Pepperberry-crusted Venison with Pickled Cherries

SERVES 4

700g–1kg venison loin, excess sinew trimmed

Salt

2 tablespoons pepperberries (or regular black peppercorns)

Olive oil

Oil, for frying

Handful of rocket

125ml (½ cup) labne (see page 246)

PICKLED CHERRIES

2 handfuls of red cherries, stems and pips removed

2 bay leaves

1 cinnamon stick

½ teaspoon whole cloves

250ml (1 cup) water

250ml (1 cup) red wine vinegar

2 tablespoons brown sugar

To make the pickled cherries, pack the cherries into a sterilised jar (see page 23) along with the bay leaves, cinnamon and cloves.

Combine the water, vinegar and sugar in a pot, stir and bring it to the boil to dissolve the sugar. Pour the hot syrup over the cherries, seal the jar while the pickling liquid is still hot and set aside to cool.

Season the venison loin with salt.

Crush the pepperberries or peppercorns in a mortar and pestle to make a coarse powder. Tip the crushed pepperberries onto a plate and add a little olive oil to help the spice to stick to the meat. Roll the loin in the pepperberries until evenly coated.

Heat a frypan over a medium–high heat, add a little cooking oil and sear the loin, turning every minute or so to ensure that the meat is coloured all over. After 4 minutes, remove the loin from the pan and let it rest for 5 minutes or so.

Make a salad with the rocket, labne and pickled cherries.

To serve, slice the loin into 5mm slices and serve with the salad, with extra pickled cherries decanted on the side.

A leg of venison is perfect for curing. The leanness of the meat means that ham can be made in a relatively short period of time, unlike a leg of pork. The resulting product is packed with salty flavour, and its firm texture is perfect when thinly sliced. All you need is a venison leg, salt, somewhere cool to hang the ham – and a whole lot of patience.

Venison Ham

MAKES 1 x 3.5KG HAM

3kg cooking salt

3.5kg venison leg, bone in

Lots of time

Lay half the salt in a plastic tub that is large enough to hold the venison. Lay the venison leg on top and pour over the remainder of the salt, massaging it into all the nooks and crannies. Place a tray that is a little smaller than the leg on top of the leg and then use something like a brick or heavy casserole dish to weigh it down. Put the curing venison in a cool place for a week.

After a week, remove the leg, flip it over and pack it in the salt again to continue curing for another week.

After that week is up, remove the leg from the salt – by this stage the meat should be very firm – and rinse it under cold water. Pat the leg dry and then find somewhere to let it hang uncovered for five months. In a perfect world, you'd have a curing room that would keep everything at a constant 12°C with 80% humidity, but a cool place with a bit of airflow, like a larder or vermin-proof shed, will do the job. The temperature needs to stay under 20°C, so if you're in a warm climate, your best bet would be to cure the meat in mid autumn and let it hang through to spring. If you're in a hot climate then you'll need to hang the meat in a temperature- and humidity-controlled environment. A bloom of white mould may form while the meat is hanging. Don't worry – this is totally harmless. Only be concerned if the mould is a funky colour or if the meat starts to develop an unpleasant smell.

Once properly cured and hung the leg will be very firm and a rich, dark red colour. Cut very thin slices as you need them and store the leg in a cool, airy place.

I love to smoke meat and I love to slow cook meat. These two methods can transform a spice-crusted beef brisket into otherworldly pastrami. It takes a while to get the job done, but when you've tasted the results you'll understand what all the fuss is about.

Pastrami

SERVES 8

Note: You need to start this recipe at least four days in advance.

1 x 1kg beef brisket, trimmed to a neat, flat slab

10g (1 heaped tablespoon) black peppercorns, crushed

10g (1 heaped tablespoon) coriander seeds, crushed

BRINE

2 litres (8 cups) water

200g cooking salt

75g caster sugar

50g honey

2 bay leaves

2 cloves garlic

1 cinnamon stick

1 teaspoon juniper berries

1 teaspoon dried chilli flakes

Combine all the brine ingredients in a large, heavy-based saucepan and bring to the boil, stirring so the sugar and salt dissolve. Remove from the heat and allow to cool.

Place the meat in an airtight container, cover with brine and refrigerate for three days.

Remove the brisket from the brine, rinse under cold water and pat dry. Discard the brine. Massage the crushed peppercorns and coriander seeds into the brined brisket, pressing them in firmly. Cover the brisket and let it stand in the fridge for a day.

Fire up a cold smoker and smoke the brisket for 2 hours. (See smoked trout, page 111, to find out more about a cold smoker.)

Preheat your oven to 120°C. Put a little water in the bottom of a large baking tray and place a wire rack lined with foil on top. Lay the smoked brisket on the rack and cover the whole tray with foil. Cook for 3 hours, making certain that the water in the tray doesn't completely evaporate. The pastrami is ready when it easily yields under the tip of a knife.

You can serve it hot or at room temperature. Slice the pastrami thinly across the grain and layer thickly on homemade rye bread (see page 223) with pickled cucumbers and a dollop of Dijon mustard.

The idea of eating raw red meat may conjure up images of early humans tucking into woolly mammoth cutlets. The reality, however, can be considerably more sophisticated. The finest beef fillet, minced with a sharp knife and with the addition of a few flavour-packed ingredients, results in something far greater than the sum of its parts. Serve the garnishes separately so that everyone can be the master of their own beef-tartare adventure.

Beef Tartare

SERVES 4

400g high-quality, grass-fed beef fillet

2 teaspoons Dijon mustard

Splash of cognac

Splash of Tabasco

Salt and pepper

4 free-range egg yolks

Crusty white bread, toasted, to serve

GARNISH

4 cornichons, finely sliced

4 white anchovies, finely sliced

2 shallots, finely sliced

1 tablespoon baby capers, rinsed

Small bunch of flat-leaf parsley, finely chopped

Small bunch of chives, finely chopped

Salt flakes and pepper

Using a *very* sharp knife, cut 5mm slices of the beef fillet. Cut those slices into matchsticks and in turn cut the matchsticks into a fine dice. Place the beef into a mixing bowl and add the Dijon, cognac and Tabasco, season with a little salt and pepper and mix it together.

Divide the beef among four small plates, shaping each portion into a neat mound. Make a small indent in each mound and top with an egg yolk. Serve with a couple of slices of lightly toasted crusty white bread.

For the garnish, place each ingredient in a small, individual bowl or plate. Each person can then add whatever garnishes they please and create their own unique tartare experience by mashing it all together on their own plate.

Portable, delicious and filling, a good burger is the ultimate two-handed hunger buster. Steer clear of lean mince for your burger making; instead favour mince from cuts like the chuck, brisket and short rib — the fat helps provide moisture and flavour. In my experience, cattle breeds with high levels of marbling, like Jersey and Wagyu beef, make the juiciest burgers.

Classic Jersey Beef Burgers

SERVES 4

1 brown onion, finely diced

Oil, for frying

1kg minced Jersey or Wagyu veal (though any high-quality, non-lean beef mince will suffice)

1 free-range egg

1 tablespoon Dijon mustard

Salt and pepper

Cheddar cheese (optional)

4 milk buns (see page 224) or soft burger buns

Homemade mayonnaise (see page 38) or some store-bought mayo

2 leaves of mustard greens, roughly chopped (or you could use any non-bitter lettuce leaf)

1 baby cos lettuce

Tomato relish

Put the onions and a little oil in a frypan on a medium heat and sauté the onions for a couple of minutes until they are soft and golden. Set aside to cool.

In a large mixing bowl combine the mince, egg and Dijon mustard, and season generously with salt and pepper. Once the onion has cooled, add it to the mince mixture and give the whole thing a good mix with your hands.

Heat a frypan, add a little oil and test the seasoning of the burger mixture by making a tiny pattie and cooking it. If everything is to your liking then proceed to shape up four burgers.

Using the same frypan, cook the burgers over a medium heat for 3 or 4 minutes per side until they are well browned and a little pink in the middle (if you like them medium rare).

Once I've turned my burgers I like to lay a couple of thin slices of Cheddar on top of the patties so the heat melts the cheese.

To serve, cut the milk buns in half and lightly toast. Slather both sides with a bit of mayo, then arrange the mustard greens and cos leaves on the bottom halves, place the cooked burger on top, finish with a dollop of tomato relish and enjoy.

If you've ever been to a footy game, you could easily jump to the conclusion that the gods blessed Australian men with two hands for a reason – one hand for holding a beer and the other for holding a pie. It's a stereotype, I know, but on a cold winter's day there is nothing better than beef and beer. Wrap the two together in a pastry shell and your other hand is free for gesturing abuse at referees.

Jersey Beef and Stout Pie

SERVES 6

75g (½ cup) plain flour

Salt and pepper

1kg Jersey beef chuck steak (or other high-quality beef chuck steak), cut into 2cm cubes

Oil, for frying

2 brown onions, finely diced

3 carrots, finely diced

3 garlic cloves, minced

500ml (2 cups) dark beer

500ml (2 cups) beef stock (see page 209)

1 bay leaf

Small bunch of thyme

2 sheets of frozen shortcrust pastry, thawed

2 sheets of frozen puff pastry, thawed

1 free-range egg, whisked with a splash of milk for egg wash

Sprinkle of poppy seeds

Tomato sauce, to serve

Put the flour into a deep-sided tray and season generously with salt and pepper. Toss in the beef cubes and shake the tray so the meat is evenly coated.

Heat some oil in a large casserole dish over a medium–high heat. Shake any excess flour off the beef and pop it into the pan. Sear the meat for around 5–10 minutes so that it has a golden crust but is raw in the centre, then set aside. Cook the meat in batches so that you don't overcrowd the pan and cause the beef to stew rather than fry.

Using the same pan, add a touch more oil and sauté the onion and carrots until lightly coloured, add the garlic and cook until soft and fragrant. Pour in the beer and use a wooden spoon to scrape up any crusty bits from the bottom of the pan.

Add the beef stock, bay and thyme and return the beef to the pan. Bring to a gentle simmer and cover. Cook for around an hour and a half or until the sauce is thick and the meat is falling apart. Take the pan off the heat, remove the bay leaf and thyme and allow to cool.

Preheat the oven to 190°C and lightly grease a 30cm pie tin.

While the filling is cooling, place the shortcrust pastry sheets over the pie tin, cutting them as needed to fit. Where the sheets overlap, brush a little water along the edge of the lower sheet and press the sheets together. Push the pastry to fit the base and sides of the tin and then place it in the fridge to rest for 15 minutes. After it's rested, trim any excess pastry.

Spoon the filling into the pie tin lined with the shortcrust pastry.

Use a pastry brush to paint the rim of the pie with the egg wash, then lay the puff pastry over the top, pressing down on the edges to seal. If you're feeling a little fancy you can cut another strip of pastry and crimp it around the edge for better presentation. Brush the puff pastry with the remaining egg wash and prick the top a couple of times with a knife to let any steam escape. Scatter over some poppy seeds and pop it in the oven.

Cook for 20–25 minutes, or until the shortcrust pastry is golden. When it's cooked the pie should easily lift away from the pie tin. Allow to cool a little, then serve with tomato sauce.

A winter must! Beef daube epitomises everything that is awesome about the alchemy of slow cooking. You begin with cheap, tough cuts of meat and with a little help from a gentle heat, some aromatics and a lot of time they are transformed into small pieces of heaven. Save this one for a lazy winter weekend. Marinate the beef on Friday night and start cooking on Saturday morning, letting the steamy aromas fill the kitchen. If you possess a will of iron, let your daube cool and then enjoy for Sunday lunch or, if you're like me, get a big pot of mash on for a late Saturday lunch and tuck in the second that the meat is tender (after all, you can always let the leftovers infuse for Sunday).

Beef Daube

SERVES 4

1kg grass-fed chuck steak, cut into 3cm cubes

Salt and pepper

375ml (½ bottle) red wine

Oil, for frying

200g air-cured bacon, such as pancetta, cut into batons

1 brown onion, diced

1 carrot, diced

4 garlic cloves, finely chopped

250ml (1 cup) passata (see page 64)

250ml (1 cup) beef stock (see page 209)

1 bay leaf

A few sprigs of thyme

Knob of butter

Small bunch of flat-leaf parsley, finely chopped

Season the chuck steak generously with salt and pepper. Place the steak in a deep-sided, plastic container and pour over the red wine. Cover and refrigerate overnight, turning the meat as often as you like.

The next day, remove the steak from the red wine marinade and pat dry. Reserve the liquid for later in the recipe.

Place a casserole dish with a tight-fitting lid on the stove on a medium–high heat. Add a little oil to the dish and fry the beef in as many batches as required, making sure that it's never too tightly packed and that the meat is nicely browned all over. Place the beef to one side and then add the pancetta batons to the casserole dish, frying until they are coloured all over.

Next, add the diced onion and carrot and cook, stirring occasionally, until they soften and start to colour. Add the garlic and continue cooking until it has softened. Pour the reserved red wine marinade into the casserole dish and use a wooden spoon to scrape up any crusty bits. Simmer for a minute or two then add the beef, passata and beef stock, along with the bay leaf and thyme.

Place the lid on the casserole dish and simmer over a very low heat for 3 hours. You'll know that it's done when the beef is meltingly tender and the sauce is rich.

To finish, season with salt and pepper, gently stir a knob of butter through the sauce until it has emulsified and sprinkle the dish with finely chopped parsley.

You can serve this straight from the stovetop onto a bed of creamy mash potato or polenta, though the daube will benefit from a night or two in the fridge to allow the flavours to mature.

There are few pieces of meat that inspire more awe, *ohhs* and *ahhs* around a dining table than a big, glistening, standing rib roast. A generous covering of fat keeps the joint moist while it roasts and the bone adds even more flavour to this delicious cut. Whip this one out when you want to wow a crowd of hungry guests but you don't want to spend all day in the kitchen.

Standing Rib Roast

SERVES 6

5-rib (2.5–3kg) standing rib roast

Olive oil

Salt flakes and pepper

Small bunch of thyme, leaves picked and finely chopped

Remove the meat from the fridge at least an hour before you're roasting it so that the beef can come up to room temperature.

Preheat the oven to 220°C.

Lightly score the fat of the beef and massage with olive oil, salt, pepper and the thyme leaves. Transfer to a rack that is set over a roasting pan and place in the oven.

Roast for 25 minutes and then lower the oven temperature to 180°C and, depending on the size of your rib roast, continue cooking for another hour and 15 minutes to an hour and 45 minutes, or until the internal temperature reaches 55°C for rare beef. (When cooking big joints of meat like this, a probe thermometer helps take out the guesswork. Make sure you insert the thermometer in the thickest part of the meat but away from the bone.)

Cover the meat to keep it warm and rest it for 30 minutes, then carve.

Serve with horseradish cream, steamed baby spuds and a leafy salad from the garden.

There is something about eating ribs that satisfies my soul on a deep, primal level. It might be the soft, sticky meat that pulls straight off the bone or the little pile of denuded bones that you're left with at the end. Whatever the reason, slow-cooked pork ribs are definitely one of my all-time favourite meals. Throw in the fact that ribs are a cheap, secondary cut of meat and there's even more reason to grab some from your local butcher and call a couple of mates over to indulge their inner cave man.

Braised and Barbecued Pork Spare Ribs

SERVES 4

4 sets (about 2.5kg) pork spare ribs

330ml apple cider

2 litres (8 cups) chicken stock (see page 208) or water

1 large brown onion, roughly chopped

4 garlic cloves, roughly chopped

4 cloves

2 bay leaves

Salt flakes, to serve

BARBECUE SAUCE

Oil, for frying

1 medium brown onion, roughly chopped

5 large garlic cloves, roughly chopped

4 coriander roots, cleaned and scraped

125ml (½ cup) passata (see page 64)

60ml (¼ cup) apple cider vinegar

90g (¼ cup) molasses

50g (¼ cup) brown sugar

1 tablespoon smoked paprika

2 teaspoons ground cumin

2 teaspoons hot English mustard

2 tablespoons Worcestershire sauce

1 teaspoon salt

½–1 teaspoon cayenne pepper

Preheat your oven to 170°C.

Put the pork ribs, cider, stock (or water), onion, garlic, cloves and bay leaves in a deep-sided roasting tray. Cover the tray securely with foil and braise in the oven for 1½ –2 hours or until the ribs are tender. While they're cooking, make your sauce.

To make the barbecue sauce, heat a medium-sized saucepan over a low heat. Add a little oil, then fry the onion and garlic gently for a few minutes until the onion is softened but not browned. Crush the coriander roots in a mortar and pestle and add to the pot along with the rest of the ingredients. Stir well to combine, raise the heat and simmer for 10 minutes. The sauce is now ready for basting.

Once the ribs are cooked in the oven, preheat a grill or a barbecue to a medium–high heat. Generously baste the ribs with the sauce, then grill them until the sauce caramelises and they're sticky and crusty. Serve with extra sauce on the side.

With a hot wok and a few simple ingredients you can whip up this tasty Laotian salad in a flash. Lime, fish sauce, aromatic herbs and chilli lift the wok-fried pork mince to create a palate-pleasing dish that packs a serious flavour punch.

Pork Larb

SERVES 4

2 tablespoons fish sauce

60ml (¼ cup) chicken stock (see page 208) or pork stock

1 tablespoon rapadura or brown sugar

Peanut or rice bran oil, for frying

750g high-quality, free-range pork mince

6 lemon myrtle or kaffir lime leaves, finely sliced

A few coriander roots, scraped and finely chopped

2 garlic cloves, finely sliced

1 medium red onion, finely sliced

1 mild red chilli, finely sliced

Small handful of purple basil, chopped

Small handful of mint, chopped

Juice of 2 limes

Small bunch of coriander, roughly chopped

Combine the fish sauce, stock and sugar in a bowl, stirring to dissolve the sugar.

Heat a large wok over a high heat and add a little cooking oil. Once the oil is hot, chuck in the pork mince and stir-fry for 3–4 minutes until brown. Add the lemon myrtle (or kaffir lime leaves), coriander root and garlic and stir-fry for a further 2 minutes until aromatic.

Add the fish sauce, stock and sugar mix to the wok and cook for 1 minute. Stir through the onion and chilli and then remove the wok from the heat.

Stir through the basil and mint leaves and then the lime juice, and top with the coriander leaves.

Serve on a bed of steamed Asian greens and rice.

This magnificent hog roast will serve an army. A small pig – say 35kg – yields enough meat for around 100 people.

Spit-roasting kits are available in various forms. The most basic is a three-piece set-up made of cast iron, with two spikes that support the spit simply hammered into the ground. The fire, ideally of wooden logs, is lit directly on the ground. A more elaborate box-basket set-up allows you to suspend the fire above the ground, and the spit above that, and is particularly good for use on hard ground such as concrete. Make sure your spit-roasting kit includes fixing skewers, which go right through the animal to be roasted, securing it on the spit so it doesn't slip round as it roasts.

It's increasingly easy to hire a spit-roasting kit – usually a gas-fired one with an electric-powered turning spit. You won't get quite such a fine flavour as you will when you wood-roast your pig, but you will save yourself a lot of time and sweat.

Hugh's Spit-roast Pig with Aromatic Crackling

SERVES AT LEAST 100

1 pig, 35–50kg dead weight, head on and split up to the neck, brought up to ambient temperature for about 12 hours (i.e. remove the meat from the fridge the night before)

6 heaped tablespoons fennel seeds

6 heaped tablespoons coriander seeds

6 heaped tablespoons salt flakes

A dozen or so bay leaves, shredded

Olive or sunflower oil

Salt and pepper

Push the point of the spit through the rear of the pig, along the inside of the cavity, into the throat and out through the mouth. It takes a bit of pushing and shoving but you'll get there in the end. Pass the fixing skewers through one side of the animal, through the holes in the spit and out through the animal's other side. Use at least four skewers, at even intervals, to fix it securely. The trotters can either be bound together, using strong wire, under the chin of the pig or bound to the last fixing skewer at the head end. The back feet, if not tucked up under the animal's belly, can either be left hanging free or bound to either end of an extra fixing skewer passed through an extra hole in the spit behind the animal's back end.

Use a sharp Stanley knife, or similar, to score the skin. Set the blade so that it's long enough to cut into the fat but not right through into the meat – just 2mm or so. Score the skin of the pig in parallel lines, about 2cm apart, across the shoulders, flanks and back, at right angles to the backbone all the way down.

Roughly bash the fennel and coriander seeds in a mortar and pestle and mix with the salt and shredded bay leaves. Massage the pig all over with a little oil, then rub the spice mix all over the pig, making sure you rub it into all the cuts as well as inside the cavity.

Once you have the fire well under way, mount the pig over it and cook, turning it regularly, for a minimum of 6 hours for a small pig – up to 10 hours for a 40–50kg pig.

Be aware that the thicker parts – i.e. the rump and shoulders – will take longer to cook so it's worth trying to maintain a fire that is hotter at the two ends than it is in the middle.

It's important to understand that the pig should be cooked by the indirect heat of the fire. The flames should never be directly under the animal (the skin would soon burn). Instead you need to create a column of heat along one or both sides of the animal, either with two parallel columns of fire or with an oval ring of fire, in each case with the animal in the middle. You can control the heat level by stoking or raking the fire and, with some kinds of spit, raising and lowering the animal. Regular turning ensures even cooking.

Acres of golden, crispy crackling are one of the great joys of a spit-roast pig, but bear in mind that the skin can burn rather easily. Hugh's technique is not to let the skin crackle too much until the pig is cooked. Then you can stoke up the fire and increase the heat to add that final, blistering, irresistible crackle. At this end stage, watch it very carefully, and speed up the frequency of your turns. Under this fierce final heat, crackling can go from golden perfection to charred disappointment in less than a minute.

When the pig is cooked (a meat thermometer inserted into the thickest part of the shoulder and rump should read at least 70°C), lift it from the fire and carry it to your carving station. Let it rest for half an hour or so before removing the skewers and the spit and digging in. Begin by pulling off all the crackling and roughly chopping it or breaking it up. Pile it on to several plates, season with a bit of salt and pepper and ask someone to pass it around. Then carve the meat into thickish slices. I think plates and cutlery are more trouble than they're worth when feeding this kind of food to large numbers so some kind of sandwich is definitely the way to go.

Hugh likes to serve the carved meat in large, buttered soft baps, with a fruity salsa or chutney. Hugh's Persimmon Coriander Salsa on page 85 is ideal.

The meat that a slowly cooked pig's head yields is rich, gelatinous and flavoursome. I can pick up a well-sized, free-range pig's head from my local butcher for just a few dollars. Ask them to cut it in two for you and you can put one of the halves in the freezer for another time. A half will make a hearty feed for four people, so not only is it delicious, it's also an extremely economical way to put quality meat on the table.

Roast Pig's Head

SERVES 4

½ a pig's head (remove hairs with a razor)

Salt and pepper

Olive oil

2 large brown onions, sliced

1 head of garlic, cloves peeled

250ml (1 cup) sherry

500ml (1 small bottle) cider

1 litre (4 cups) chicken stock (see page 208)

2 bay leaves

Small bunch of thyme

½ teaspoon black peppercorns

Preheat the oven to 140°C.

Season the pig's head generously with salt and pepper and wrap the ears in foil to stop them from burning.

Pour some olive oil into a roasting tray that is big enough to accommodate the pig's head. Put the tray on the stovetop over a medium heat, add the onion and garlic and cook gently until softened and starting to colour.

Put the head in the pan and pour over the sherry, cider and chicken stock, then add the bay leaves, thyme and peppercorns. Cover the pig's head with a sheet of baking paper and then cover the roasting tray with foil – this will keep in the moisture and prevent the skin from sticking to the foil. After 2 hours, remove the foil and the baking paper and return the head to the oven to continue roasting for another 2 hours. By this stage the skin should be rich in colour and the flesh soft and yielding.

Remove the head from the pan and transfer it to a warm plate. Enjoy straight away by picking the meat from the bone and slapping it on a crusty bread roll with a dollop of Dijon mustard.

If you eat super-fresh pork liver you'll understand just how great offal can be. A good butcher should be able to supply fresh, free-range pork liver but even that pales in comparison to the liver of a happy porker that you've raised and killed yourself. Simply sliced and quickly fried with a splash of vinegar to cut through the richness, a tasty piece of pork liver could sway even the most reluctant offal eater.

Panfried Pork Liver with Balsamic Glaze

SERVES 4

500g fresh free-range pig's liver, cut into 1cm thick slices

Salt and pepper

Oil, for frying

30g butter

5 sage leaves

2 cloves garlic, chopped

2 tablespoons balsamic vinegar

Handful of flat-leaf parsley, finely chopped

Season the liver on both sides with salt and pepper. Place a frypan over a high heat, add a little oil and fry the liver slices for about 90 seconds each side until brown on the outside but still a little pink in the middle.

Transfer the liver to a warm plate and lower the heat to medium. Pop the butter, sage and garlic in the pan and sauté until the garlic becomes soft and aromatic. Add the balsamic vinegar and let it reduce for about 30 seconds, until it starts to become syrupy. Toss in a small handful of chopped parsley and spoon the sauce over the livers.

Serve with toast spread with cultured butter (see page 240) and a simple green salad on the side.

A good blood pudding is an essential recipe to have
tucked up your sleeve. When I kill my pigs on the farm
the meat needs to be hung for at least a couple of days
before it's ready to eat. The wait is only made bearable by
the promise of the delicious pork to come and a big tray
of blood pudding to enjoy in the meantime. I know that
I'm in the minority when it comes to having access to
fresh pig's blood but any good butcher should be able to
help you out with a couple of litres of processed stuff that
will work just fine in this recipe.

Blood Pudding

SERVES 6

150g cooled, cooked rice
(overcooked is best because it
has absorbed as much liquid
as it can and will help keep the
pudding moist)

150g rolled oats

300g pork fat, cut into small
cubes

1 small brown onion, finely
diced

½ teaspoon nutmeg

½ teaspoon salt

A few grinds of pepper

1 litre (4 cups) fresh pig's blood

Preheat your oven to 175°C and grease a 40cm roasting pan.

Thoroughly mix all the ingredients, except the blood, in a large
bowl. In a separate bowl briefly whisk the blood, then pour it
over the mix through a fine sieve. Fold the blood in.

Pour the mixture into the roasting pan, making sure all the
solids are evenly distributed. Bake for 45 minutes or until a fork
or skewer inserted into the pudding comes out clean.

Remove from the oven and cool to room temperature.

To serve, cut into squares and fry until slightly crispy and
warmed through. Serve it up with some baked beans and fried
free-range eggs for a hearty brekkie or with some roasted pears
and a bitter leaf salad for something a little more sophisticated.

Keep the pudding covered and in the fridge, where it will last
for up to a week.

High-quality meat is the essential starting point for the very best bangers, and a pork shoulder provides a perfect balance between tasty lean meat and moisture-providing fat. To avoid a dry sausage, around a quarter of the sausage meat should consist of fat. Once you've mastered this simple recipe, you can experiment with any flavour that strikes your fancy.

Simple Pork Sausages

MAKES 3KG SAUSAGES

1 length of natural hog casing (ask your butcher for this)

3kg free-range, old-breed pork shoulder, deboned and skin removed

6 garlic cloves, finely chopped

3 tablespoons fennel seeds, toasted and lightly crushed

250ml (1 cup) white wine

30g salt

A good couple of twists of pepper

A little oil

To make your own sausages, you can't go past quality, Italian-made, hand-cranked mincers and sausage stuffers. They're relatively cheap and if you look after them they'll last forever. I've got a Tre Spade mincer and a Reber sausage stuffer and I can mince and stuff a shoulder's worth of pork sausages in no time.

Before starting, place all the components of the mincer in the freezer for an hour so they are ice cold. Soak the sausage casing in a big bowl of fresh water to remove any excess salt or brine.

Cut the pork into chunks small enough to fit into the hopper of the mincer. Remove any sinew or silver skin that you come across.

Remove the mincer from the freezer and mince the shoulder into a big mixing bowl. Add the garlic, fennel seeds, wine, salt and pepper. Mix it with your hands until combined and then pinch off a little bit and fry it in a small pan to check the seasoning. If everything is to your liking, then you're ready to move on to stuffing.

Rub a little oil onto the nozzle of the sausage stuffer, remove the casing from the water and then feed it onto the end of the nozzle. Once the casing is loaded, tie a small knot in the end and hold the closed casing flush to the end of the nozzle. Load the mince into the chamber of the stuffer and slowly work the mix through into the casing. Use one hand to keep a tiny bit of pressure on the casing as the mince comes through – this will help fill the sausages evenly. Too loosely packed and the sausages will be full of air pockets, too tightly packed and they'll explode when you try to twist them into links.

When all the mince has been stuffed into the casing, give the casing a couple of twists every 10cm or so to form individual sausages. I'm told that it is easy to twist your snags up into those fancy chains that you see in butcher shops, but my chains usually end up looking a bit mangled. Don't fret if your snags look a little scruffy; as long as they aren't overfilled and have no air pockets, they'll be fine. Whatever you end up with, dry them uncovered on a wire rack in the fridge for a day. Use a pin sterilised with boiling water to prick any air pockets.

The snags will keep in the fridge for a couple of days, or can be frozen for a couple of months. Cook the sausages steadily over a medium heat, turning regularly to ensure even cooking. A perfectly cooked sausage will be packed full of moisture.

Bacon is an almost universally appealing food – even my vegetarian friends say that the one thing that really tests their resolve is the smell of bacon frying. However, so much of the bacon available today is a watery, liquid-smoke infused shadow of the salty goodness that bacon can be. With a little salt, some pork belly and some patience you can easily make a slab of delicious bacon at home. The smoked paprika is a bit of a cheeky way of getting that smoky flavour without having to fire up a cold smoker.

Easy Home-cured Bacon

MAKES 3KG

Note: You need to start this recipe at least five days in advance.

4 teaspoons fennel seeds, toasted

4 teaspoons smoked paprika

Small bunch of thyme, leaves picked

300g (1 cup) cooking salt

95g (½ cup) brown sugar

3kg piece free-range pork belly, skin on, all bones removed

Grind the fennel seeds, paprika, thyme leaves, salt and sugar together to make a dry curing rub.

Lay the pork belly out on a board and trim any cartilage or loose flaps of skin away so that the surface of the flesh is nice and even. Massage the curing mix evenly into the belly, making sure that you work the mix into every nook and cranny. Place the belly onto a wire rack over a deep-sided tray, cover it with cling film and then pop it in the fridge. The salt will start to draw the moisture out of the meat almost immediately.

Empty the liquid that pools in the tray underneath the belly daily and top up with extra cure as required.

After about four days the belly should be feeling firm and cured. Rinse off the salt rub with cold water, pat dry, wrap in a piece of baking paper and store in the fridge for up to a fortnight. To serve, cut thin slices of bacon and fry over a medium heat until brown and crispy.

This classic piece of French café fare is the ultimate quick lunch or, more often than not, midnight snack. With bacon, egg, cheese, mustard, sourdough bread and a creamy chickpea-flour béchamel it ticks all the boxes for a hearty hunger buster. I love to use fried duck eggs for this recipe, as they have a higher yolk to white ratio and when you cook them just right the yolk makes a wonderful, rich, oozy sauce for the croque.

Tilba Croque Madame

MAKES 2 TOASTED SANDWICHES

2 tablespoons butter

1 tablespoon chickpea (besan) flour

180ml (¾ cup) full cream milk

130g Cheddar cheese, grated

Small bunch of chives, finely chopped

4 slices streaky bacon

4 slices sourdough bread (see pages 218–19)

Dijon mustard

Oil, for frying

2 free-range duck eggs (free-range chicken eggs are fine too)

Melt 1 tablespoon of the butter in a saucepan over a low heat, add the chickpea flour and cook for a few minutes without browning. Add the milk and cook for a further 4–5 minutes, stirring with a whisk to make sure there are no lumpy bits. Once the sauce has thickened, add the cheese and the chives and stir to combine. Remove the pan from the heat and place to one side.

Preheat your grill to hot.

Panfry the bacon to your liking, then place the bacon to one side. Keep the fat in the pan and lower the heat a little, then add the other tablespoon of butter. Fry the bread in the butter and bacon fat (dieters beware!) until both sides are golden brown.

Remove the toast from pan and lightly spread some Dijon on the top of all four slices. Place half the bacon on top of one slice and the other half on top of another and then liberally cover all four slices with the béchamel.

Place the four slices on a tray and under the hot grill until the tops are golden brown and crusty.

Meanwhile, fry your eggs in a little oil, being sure to leave the centres nice and runny.

To assemble, place the two slices of toast that have the bacon on them on serving plates, then place the remaining two slices on top, and then place a fried egg on top of each sandwich. Enjoy!

I don't have time for a cooked breakfast every day but when I do, it doesn't get much better than a flavour-packed omelette. Salty bacon, creamy labne and aromatic mint are the perfect way to wake up the taste buds and fuel up for the day.

Labne, Bacon and Mint Omelette

SERVES 4

6 free-range eggs

125ml (½ cup) double cream

Salt and pepper

Knob of butter

2 rashers of bacon
(see page 193),
cut into batons

2 spring onions, finely
sliced (green and white
parts separated)

6 tablespoons labne
(see page 246)

Several pinches of
smoked paprika

Small bunch of mint, leaves
roughly torn

Salt flakes, toast and cultured
butter (see page 240), to serve

Preheat your grill to medium.

In a bowl, whisk together the eggs, cream and a pinch of salt and pepper.

Heat a frypan over a medium heat and toss in the knob of butter. Once it's starting to foam add the bacon and the white parts of the spring onion. After 1–2 minutes, when the bacon has started to colour, add the green parts of the spring onion and cook for 30 seconds. Turn the heat up a little and then pour over the egg mixture.

When the bottom has set, crumble over the labne and sprinkle over the smoked paprika. Pop the pan under a grill to set the top, and then add the mint leaves.

Serve with some butter-soaked toast, a couple of extra twists of pepper and salt flakes for seasoning to taste.

Rabbit Rillettes

SERVES 6

1 wild rabbit, skinned, gutted,
jointed into 8 pieces

Salt and pepper

Oil, for frying

300g pork belly, rind removed,
cut into 3cm cubes

100g duck fat (see page 205)

Small bunch of thyme

3 bay leaves

4 garlic cloves, peeled

250ml (1 cup) dry white wine

½ teaspoon freshly grated
nutmeg

Crusty bread and Dijon
mustard, to serve

Preheat your oven to 140°C.

Season the rabbit pieces with a sprinkle of salt and pepper.
Place a frypan over a medium heat, add a splash of cooking oil
and then sear the rabbit pieces in the pan, turning them until
browned all over on both sides. Transfer the rabbit pieces to
a casserole dish that can fit the meat in a single layer. Keep
the frypan on the heat.

Add the pork belly cubes to the pan and brown them all over.
Transfer the pork to the casserole with the rabbit and add the
duck fat, thyme, bay leaves, garlic and white wine. The liquid
should just cover the meat but if you're a little short then top
up with some more white wine. Place the lid on the casserole
dish and pop it in the oven. Cook for 3 hours, until the meat is
meltingly tender and slides easily from the bone.

Take the casserole dish out of the oven and wait until the meat
is cool enough to handle. Using your fingers, shred the rabbit
and pork into a bowl, making sure that you get all the tasty
fat from the pork belly as well. Or if getting your hands sticky
isn't really your thing, break the meat up with a couple of forks.
Season with plenty of salt and pepper and the nutmeg.

Strain the cooking liquid from the casserole. Pour a little of it
onto the meat and stir with a wooden spoon, then keep adding
liquid and stirring until you have a coarse, pâté-like consistency
(you will need some liquid left over). Check the seasoning and
then transfer the shredded meat into a couple of small bowls
or 500ml Kilner jars (rubber-sealed jars with clip or screwtop)
that have been sterilised (see page 23). Pour a little more of the
cooking liquid on top of the meat and then cover and place in
the refrigerator overnight to help the flavours develop. Stored
in the fridge, rillettes will last for a couple of months, though
mine are always gobbled up long before that.

To serve, spread thickly on a slice of crusty bread along with
some Dijon mustard.

Some people like to spread Vegemite on their bread, others are partial to peanut butter, or jam if they're feeling fancy. Personally I think that the best thing that can grace a piece of bread is a thick slathering of buttery chicken pâté. Made with quiveringly fresh livers and enlivened with thyme and a splash of something flash, I reckon this pâté is what bread would request for its final meal.

Chicken Liver Pâté

MAKES 400G

Oil, for frying

350g (15–20) fresh, free-range chicken livers, cleaned

2 French shallots, finely chopped

60ml (¼ cup) cognac or brandy

250g butter, softened

Salt and pepper

Crusty white bread, to serve

Heat a frypan over a medium–high heat, add a little cooking oil and fry the chicken livers until well browned on the outside and pink in the middle. (If you overcook the livers the pâté will be grainy.)

Transfer the cooked livers to the bowl of a food processor.

Add a touch more oil to the pan, and cook the shallots for about 3 minutes or until they have softened. Pour over the cognac or brandy and continue cooking until it has reduced by half, then transfer the contents of the pan to the food processor with the livers. Add 150g of the softened butter to the food processor, season with a little salt and pepper and give it all a good whiz until it's smooth.

To make sure that the finished pâté has a velvety texture, use a spatula to push the mixture through a very fine sieve. Transfer the pâté to a ceramic bowl. Enjoy straight away, spread thickly on a piece of crusty bread such as baguette (see page 220).

If you want to enjoy the pâté later take the remaining 100g of butter and slowly melt it in a small saucepan until the golden liquid and milk solids separate. Pour the golden clarified butter over the pâté so that it is totally covered and then place in the fridge to set. The pâté will keep in the fridge for up to a week, or two weeks with the clarified butter seal.

A galantine is a classic French dish that involves deboning a bird, stuffing it with all kinds of tasty bits, rolling it up, cooking it and then serving it cold. It does take some knife skills to debone a chook, but don't let that step put you off attempting this mouth-watering picnic treat. And you can always ask your friendly butcher to do it for you. You'll also need muslin and some kitchen twine to secure your boned and stuffed chicken.

Chicken Galantine with Pistachio and Lemon

SERVES 4

Oil, for frying

2 brown onions, finely chopped

2 garlic cloves, finely chopped

60ml (¼ cup) apple cider vinegar

1 small free-range, pasture-fed chicken, deboned

Salt and pepper

Small handful of tarragon leaves, finely chopped

Small handful of flat-leaf parsley leaves, finely chopped

4 sage leaves, finely chopped

Zest of 1 lemon

60g (½ cup) pistachio nuts, toasted and chopped

1½ litres (6 cups) chicken stock (see page 208)

Crusty white bread, Dijon mustard and cornichons, to serve

Heat a medium frypan over a medium–low heat, add a little oil and the onion and garlic and sauté until until they are soft and starting to turn golden, about 8–10 minutes. Add the apple cider vinegar and let it reduce until it's almost evaporated. Remove the pan from the heat and set aside to cool.

Lay the boned chicken, skin-side down, on a board. Season the inside with salt and pepper.

Spread the tarragon, parsley and sage evenly on the inside of the chicken, then layer over the onion mixture and lemon zest, and scatter over the toasted pistachios.

Roll the chicken into a cylinder, with the skin on the outside. Wrap the cylinder firmly in muslin and then bind it using kitchen twine. Transfer it to a large stockpot and pour in the cold chicken stock. Gently bring the stock to a simmer and poach the chicken gently for 30–40 minutes. Use a meat thermometer to check the internal temperature; the chicken is cooked when it reaches 72°C.

Let the galantine cool to room temperature, then put it in the fridge. When cold, remove the muslin, slice thickly and serve with crusty white bread, Dijon mustard and cornichons.

There are few things in the world that make me wiggle my toes with glee more than the thought of cooking with duck fat. I was told once by a very serious French chef that fat is flavour, and that fat from a duck (or better yet, a goose) is the king of fats. You can use it for loads of things, like slow cooking tough cuts of meat, frying your eggs for breakfast, enriching gravy or, my favourite, roasting the ultimate crispy potato. You can buy rendered duck fat from specialty food outlets, though this pales in comparison to the fat from a couple of ducks that you've reared yourself. If you don't have your own ducks then seek out free-range birds that have a nice covering of fat.

Rendered Duck Fat

MAKES ABOUT 1 LITRE

The fat from the body cavities and frames of 2 ducks or 1 goose

Water, as needed

Clear all the fat that you can from the neck, body cavity and frame of a couple of freshly killed ducks and pop it in a saucepan.

Pour in enough cold water to cover the fat and bring to a simmer. Keep that pot simmering away for about an hour or until all the water has evaporated. What you're left with is the golden nectar of the gods themselves – freshly rendered duck fat. Strain through a fine sieve and store in the fridge in an airtight jar, where it will keep for months.

A lot of enticing smells waft out of the kitchen – baking bread, a simmering stock, gently frying garlic, lemons being zested ... the list goes on. There is one aroma, however, that generates more excitement in my house than any other – the smell of salt-cured duck simmering in a bath of its own fat. It may sound a little macabre but the richly flavoured, tender meat that emerges from that fat after hours of slow cooking is heaven for the taste buds. I usually have a whole bird from the farm that I joint so that I'm left with the legs, breasts and frame. I render the excess fat from the frame and cavity and use that to cook the legs. If you can't render your own duck fat, pick some up from a quality providore or butcher.

Duck Confit

SERVES 4

100g salt

Small bunch of thyme

Zest of 1 orange

1 bay leaf

½ teaspoon juniper berries

4 duck legs

400g duck fat (see page 205)

Combine the salt, thyme, orange zest, bay leaf and juniper berries in a bowl.

Scatter half of the salt mix over the bottom of a small, deep-sided tray, lay the legs on top and scatter over the remaining salt. Massage the salt into all the nooks and crannies to get an even covering. Cover the tray with cling wrap and refrigerate overnight.

Preheat the oven to 100°C.

Remove the duck from the salt and rinse well with cold water. Pat the legs dry using a paper towel and place in a single layer in a roasting pan. Melt the duck fat in a saucepan over a medium heat and then pour over the legs so that they are completely submerged. If you don't have enough duck fat you can always cheat and top it up with a little cooking oil. Cook in the oven for at least 2 hours. You can tell the duck is cooked when the meat comes easily away from the bone.

If using straight away, remove the legs from the oil, allow to cool and then shred the meat through a salad of endive, croutons, pear and goat's curd. Or you could whack it between two buttered slices of sourdough along with some Cheddar cheese and cook it up in a jaffle maker. Reserve the fat for another time by pouring it through a fine strainer and keeping it in the fridge.

If you want to use the legs later, allow them to cool in the pan until the fat solidifies, cover the tray and place in the fridge until required. When you are ready to eat the duck legs, dig them out of the fat and place them on a tray in a 180°C oven for 10 minutes to melt away the cold, excess fat. The legs should be hot to the touch and heated all the way through, and you can reserve the melted fat to use another time.

If you haven't acquainted yourself with the joy of making your own stock then there is no time like the present to grab a big pot and get simmering. There is a particular joy that comes from the thriftiness of making your own stock – the long, slow simmering process extracts the maximum flavour and nutrients from scraps and bones. A small bank of chicken and beef stock in the freezer is essential for adding extra flavour and body to soup, gravy and risotto. For clear, clean-tasting stocks, be sure to simmer very gently and skim regularly.

Chicken Stock

MAKES ABOUT 2 LITRES

1 chicken frame (neck and feet as well if you have them!)

Water, as needed

1 brown onion, peeled and roughly diced

1 carrot, roughly diced

1 stick celery, roughly diced

1 head of garlic, cut in half horizontally

1 bay leaf

A few sprigs of thyme

½ teaspoon black peppercorns

Place the chicken frame in a stockpot and pour over about 2 litres of cold water, just enough to cover. Gently bring the water to a simmer, skimming away any impurities as they rise to the surface – use a ladle and a circular swirling motion to push them to the edge of the pot for convenient scooping.

Add the veggies, bay leaf, thyme and peppercorns and continue to gently simmer for 1½ hours. By this stage the stock should have a rich chicken flavour.

Ladle the stock through a fine strainer, allow it to come down to room temperature and then place it in the fridge, uncovered, to cool completely. Use within a couple of days or freeze it in convenient portion sizes for longer life.

Beef Stock

MAKES ABOUT 6 LITRES

**3kg meaty beef bones
(ask your butcher nicely to cut
them into manageable pieces)**

Water, as needed

**2 brown onions, peeled and
roughly diced**

2 carrots, roughly diced

2 celery sticks, roughly diced

**1 head of garlic, cut in half
horizontally**

375ml (½ bottle) red wine

2 bay leaves

A few sprigs of thyme

1 teaspoon black peppercorns

Preheat the oven to 220°C and roast the bones in a roasting pan for roughly half an hour or until browned all over.

Once the bones are brown, transfer them to a stockpot and add just enough cold water to immerse them – this should be about 7 litres. Gently bring the water to a simmer, skimming off any impurities as they rise to the surface using a ladle and a circular swirling motion.

Meanwhile, pour off and discard any excess oil from the roasting pan. Add the veggies to the pan, returning it to the oven for 15 minutes so they can get a bit of colour. Once sufficiently caramelised, remove the veggies from the pan and add to the stockpot with the bones.

Pour any remaining oil out of the roasting pan and place it on the stove over a medium heat. Pour in the wine and use a wooden spoon to scrape up any lovely crusty bits from the bottom of the pan. Simmer for a couple of minutes and then pour this into the pot with the bones and veggies.

Add the bay leaves, thyme and black peppercorns to the pot and cook just below a simmer for 12 hours, skimming as often as you think of it. If the level of the liquid falls below the bones, top up with a little cold water. Ladle the stock through a fine strainer and allow it to come to room temperature before placing it in the fridge, uncovered, to cool. Use within a couple of days or freeze it in convenient portion sizes for longer life.

BREAD

Bread has been filling our bellies in some form or another since the Stone Age. Ancient millstones discovered in Europe and Australia suggest that wild seeds and grains were harvested and then ground to make a basic flour long before the spread of agricultural practices and the domestication of wheat. Grinding up otherwise unpalatable seeds and roots into flour, mixing it with water and baking it is, like hunting an animal and cooking it on a fire, one of our most ancient forms of cookery. Was it these ancient breads that heralded a shift away from animal proteins and fats as the staple food source of a hunter-gatherer, towards a more cereal-dependent diet and the adoption of agriculture? That question is best left to archaeologists and anthropologists. However, one thing that is certain is that bread has stood the test of time, and remains not just a cornerstone of our diet, but of our culture.

We've come a long way since those Stone Age flat breads, though the basic ingredients remain relatively unchanged: flour, water, yeast and salt. As far as ingredient lists go it doesn't get much more basic than that. Through the millennia clever bakers have come up with a dizzying array of breads, which all revolve around those four central ingredients. Some, like a loaf of sourdough from a skilful baker, will have changed little in appearance or flavour and would be as familiar to a Roman centurion as they are to a modern urbanite.

Unfortunately, though, the majority of bread both baked and consumed today is a pale shadow of the nutritious loaves that have sustained our societies for centuries. Modern industrial baking techniques rely heavily on inferior ingredients, machinery and additives, sacrificing nutrition, texture and flavour in favour of profits. Happily there has been a proliferation in recent years of bakers who care about their craft, and a good loaf is never far away. For the ultimate in bread satisfaction, however, lovingly baking your own loaf is the only way to go. It may take a little time, you may make a little mess, but the pay off is that with just four simple ingredients you can create something that is far greater than the sum of its parts. But be warned – baking your own bread is addictive. Once you smell and taste your first freshly baked loaf, the stuff from the shop, no matter how good the baker, will never be able to compare.

A good loaf of bread is built on the best ingredients – you can't bake a superior loaf with inferior ingredients. With that in mind, I always have a store of quality bread-baking essentials in the pantry. If you're new to the baking world, the many different types of flour and yeast may be a little confusing. Here's a quick guide to the basics.

UNBLEACHED ORGANIC STONEGROUND WHEAT FLOUR WITH A PROTEIN CONTENT OF 12-14%

I like to keep a good stock of both white and wholemeal flours, as they can be used either individually or mixed to make delicious loaves.

The stone-grinding process slowly crushes the whole-wheat grain, retaining maximum nutrition through a low processing temperature. For wholemeal flour, nothing else is done and the flour has flecks of the crushed bran through it, adding texture and flavour.

To make white flour, the millers sieve the flour as it's ground to remove as much of the bran and germ as possible, while keeping the white flour from the ground endosperm (which is the pale interior of the grain that makes up the bulk of the weight). Stoneground flour is never really 'white' in the way that its bleached, roller-milled counterpart is, but what it lacks in pure colour it amply compensates for with flavour and nutrition.

You've probably also heard bakers talking about soft or hard flour. They're talking about how much protein is in the flour, with a soft flour typically having 7–10% protein and hard flour having 12–14% protein. Of that protein content, approximately 80% is gluten and, love it or loathe it, gluten is what allows bread to rise and gives it structure and shape. This means that for cakes and the like you'd use a soft flour – usually labelled 'plain flour' – but for bread your best bet is to go for a hard flour, with the central north of New South Wales and the central south of Queensland growing the best high-protein flours in Australia. If you can't find good flour in your local area, there are plenty of online retailers who can get great quality Australian flour to you (see Directory, page 311).

Don't worry if you don't have self-raising flour in the cupboard. With a little baking powder on hand you can kill two birds with one stoneground flour. Simply add 3g of baking powder for every 100g of plain flour.

ORGANIC STONEGROUND RYE FLOUR

Closely related to the wheat version, rye flour has a fruity flavour, is naturally lower in gluten than wheat flour and features heavily in the bread making of Northern and Eastern European cultures. The lower gluten content gives loaves baked with rye flour a heavier texture and for the amateur baker it's easiest to mix rye flour with a little wheat flour to help improve the structure of a loaf. That said, with a little practice and the right technique, a delicious and hearty 100% rye loaf can be made.

ORGANIC STONEGROUND SPELT FLOUR

A form of ancient wheat, spelt has a sweet, nutty flavour that makes wonderful bread. As with rye, for the inexperienced baker it's easiest to start off blending it with a little wheat flour and as your baking abilities grow you can move towards a 100% spelt loaf.

YEAST

Long before scientists discovered yeast, bakers had been cultivating it to raise their dough and improve the texture of their bread. You can cultivate your own yeast in the form of a sourdough starter and I've outlined the simple and ancient technique in this chapter. The wild yeasts colonise the starter and convert naturally occurring sugars in the flour into ethanol and carbon dioxide; this helps raise the dough and gives it the distinct sour flavour. If you don't have the time or inclination to look after your own sourdough culture then fear not, because there are commercially available yeasts for baking. The easiest to come by, and the one that I keep in the cupboard as an alternative to my sourdough starter, is instant yeast. A granulated form of live yeast, it keeps in the cupboard for yonks and can be added directly to dough to make many different and delicious loaves.

There is so much to know about bread making that there is no way I can cover it all in this chapter. Baking good bread is a skill that takes a bit of practice to master, though once you get the hang of it you'll never want to buy bread from the shops again. I hope that with this little bit of info and the recipes in this chapter, I can demystify bread baking enough to encourage you to get your hands sticky with dough and to slide out of the oven that first magnificent loaf of bread.

Long before supermarkets and store-bought dried yeast were available, bakers would take advantage of the natural yeasts that are found in the air and in flour to leaven their bread. Often it was just a case of tossing a chunk of yesterday's dough into a fresh dough and letting the yeasts colonise and raise the new dough. The yeast would be kept alive, being passed from dough to dough, strengthening in resilience and flavour.

You can use any bread flour to make a starter but I find that a combination of spelt, wheat and rye makes for a lively, healthy 'mother' dough. Of course, you could also make a starter from any of these flours individually – experiment and find out which combination of flours works best for you. It will take between seven and ten days to establish a starter.

Sourdough Starter

About 150g (1 cup) whole wheat flour

About 115g (1 cup) spelt flour

About 100g (1 cup) rye flour

Note: The exact measurements for the starter don't really matter. You just need to work with roughly equal amounts of each flour.

Warm water, as needed

Combine the flours in a mixing bowl. Slowly whisk in warm water until you have a thick, batter-like consistency. That's it. You've provided the wild yeasts with everything they need to get to work, so now it's time to kick back and wait for the magic to unfold.

Cover your newborn culture with a tea towel and leave it somewhere warm. Every day, over the next seven days, remove and discard half the starter and keep adding half a cup of flour (whichever type you like) and enough water to retain its thick consistency.

After seven days (though it may take up to ten depending on the flour you are using and the conditions in which you keep your starter), you should have a mix that smells sweet and yeasty. Transfer your new culture to a container with a tight-fitting lid. Now you're ready to start making your bread.

To make your bread, you will only need a ladleful or so of starter, so you'll need to find a place to store the remainder, being sure to replenish what you use with a little more flour and water.

If you plan on baking most days you can keep your starter out of the fridge, using it and feeding it every day or so. If you're more of an irregular baker it's best to keep the starter in the fridge; the cold conditions keep the flora in the starter dormant and you'll only need to feed it every week or so.

Treat your sourdough starter right and feed it properly, and you will have good bread for years to come.

Once your sourdough starter is happily bubbling away and smelling sweet and yeasty, it's time to try your hand at baking your first loaf of sourdough. First you need to mix up what bakers call a 'sponge'. This is a wet, loose dough that allows the starter culture to multiply to a level where it can raise a loaf to bake. I like to get my sponges on before going to bed and bake the loaves in the morning. A tangy slice of freshly baked sourdough, slathered in cultured butter made with Jersey cream (see page 240), will always guarantee a feeling of deep satisfaction.

Sourdough Loaf

MAKES 1 BIG LOAF OR 2 SMALL LOAVES

SPONGE

500g (4 cups) hard white bread flour

650ml warm water

A ladleful of sourdough starter (see page 216)

DOUGH

600g (4¾ cups) hard white bread flour

25g salt

Extra flour, or semolina, for dusting

To make the sponge, mix the flour, water and starter together in a bowl. Cover and leave in a warm place until it is slightly aerated and spongy looking. This should take about 8 hours, so I usually mix it up just before I go to bed – that way, in the morning the sponge is ready and I can start making my dough.

Once your sponge is ready, add the remaining flour and salt and bring it together to form a sticky dough. Turn this out onto a floured work surface and knead it by pushing into the dough powerfully with the heels of your hands and then forward along the bench to stretch it. Fold the dough back on itself, rotate it a quarter turn and repeat. Keep kneading until the dough is smooth and satiny (10 minutes or so).

Shape the dough into a round loaf shape and put it in a lightly oiled bowl; cover with a tea towel, and place it somewhere warm for half an hour or until the dough has doubled in size. Allowing the bread to rise is known as 'proving'.

Once the dough has risen, turn it out onto a floured bench and using the tips of your fingers push down on the dough until all the air has been knocked out (bread-baking types call this 'knocking back'). Shape the dough into a round loaf, return it to the bowl, cover it and leave it to rise until doubled in size again. Repeat the process of knocking back two more times. This will take a couple of hours.

After you have knocked the air out of the dough the third time, you're nearly ready to bake. If you want to make two smaller loaves, divide the dough and shape it into the type of loaf you'd like. If you want one big loaf, that's fine too. I personally prefer longer, oval loaves, but round loaves work just as well.

Once your loaves are shaped, place them on a floured board, give them a nice dusting of flour or semolina, cover with a tea towel and allow to rise until they feel light and airy (around 45 minutes).

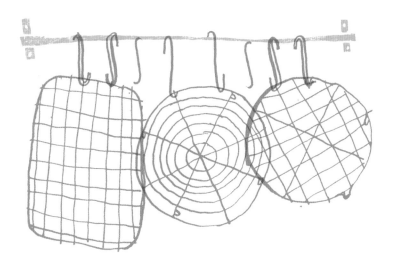

When the loaves are almost ready, switch the oven on to very high (about 250°C) and place the tray you plan to bake on in the oven. I also put a tray of water in the bottom of the oven; this will create steam and helps to give your loaf a beautiful, brown crust.

When your bread is ready to bake, remove the bread tray from the oven and quickly transfer the bread onto it. Use a serrated or sharp knife to slash the tops of the loaves and return the tray to the oven. After 10 minutes, check the bread and turn it down to 200°C if the crust is pale or 180°C if it is noticeably browning.

The bread should be ready after about 40 minutes. You can tell when a loaf is finished by tapping it firmly on the base – it should sound hollow. If your bread is starting to get too brown and still doesn't sound hollow, turn the oven down another 20°C and bake until ready. If you're in doubt always leave it a little longer – it's better for a loaf to be over-baked and crusty than under-baked, doughy and inedible.

Once the bread is baked, leave it to cool on a wire rack for 15 minutes before slicing.

I love the smell of a freshly baked loaf of bread coming out of the oven – it sends me into a childish state of anticipation. A good baguette recipe is a must in your baking repertoire. Baguettes make a mean sandwich, soak up braises and soups with a thirsty passion, are a natural partner for charcuterie and make delicious, crunchy croutons. They're also an ideal place to start for first-time bread bakers as they only require a few readily available ingredients, a little mixing and a bit of time.

Baguette

MAKES 2 x 50CM BAGUETTES

500g (4 cups) hard white bread flour

1 x 7g sachet dried yeast

10g salt

300ml warm water

Semolina for dusting

Put the flour, yeast and salt in a large mixing bowl, placing the salt and yeast on opposite sides so they don't touch. Pour in the water and mix together with your hands until a dough is formed.

Turn the wet dough out onto a lightly floured workbench and knead it by pushing strongly into the dough with the heels of your hands to stretch it. Fold the dough back on itself, rotate it a quarter turn and repeat. Knead until the dough is smooth in texture – this will take around 10 minutes. Shape your dough into a ball and transfer to a lightly oiled bowl. Cover it with a clean tea towel and put it in a warm place for around half an hour, or until the dough has doubled in size. A nice sunny windowsill or a bench next to the oven is perfect.

When the dough has risen, turn it out onto a floured bench and gently knock all the air out with the tips of your fingers. Reshape the dough into a ball and leave it to double in size again.

Preheat the oven to 240°C. Place a deep-sided baking tray half-filled with water in the bottom of the oven. This creates steam, which helps give the baguettes a light, beautiful golden crust.

When the dough has risen again, turn it out onto the bench and knock the air out again. Divide the dough into two portions and roll each portion into a cylinder shape. Transfer to a floured board and allow to prove in a warm place, covered in a tea towel, for about half an hour. The loaves are ready to bake when they feel light and delicate.

Place a baking tray in the oven until it's really hot – this helps the bread 'kick' so that it will rise well and have a nice, fluffy texture.

Remove the tray from the oven and dust it with semolina. Transfer the proven loaves to the hot oven tray, spray with a little water and lightly slash the tops with a sharp knife. Sprinkle with semolina and bake in the oven for 15 minutes. Reduce the heat to 180°C and bake for a further 20 minutes, or until the loaf is golden brown and sounds hollow when tapped.

Place on a wire rack and leave until completely cool before slicing.

Rye bread is darker and denser than breads made entirely with wheat flour. The rye adds a rich, nutty and slightly sweet flavour. The honey complements the sweetness of the rye flour and adds an extra depth of flavour to the loaf. All in all, this is just right to serve with some smoky, cured meat and a sharp Cheddar cheese.

Rye Bread

MAKES 1 LARGE LOAF

400g (3¾ cups) rye flour

500g (4 cups) hard white bread flour, plus extra for dusting

1 teaspoon salt

1 x 7g sachet dried yeast

600ml warm water

3 tablespoons honey

Combine the flours in a large mixing bowl, and then add the salt and yeast. Place them on opposite sides of the bowl so they don't touch.

In a separate bowl or jug combine the warm water and honey. Pour the honey and water mix over the flours and mix to form a sticky dough. Tip the whole lot out onto a floured work surface and knead the dough. To knead, push the dough firmly away from you with the heels of your hands to stretch it, then fold it back on itself and rotate it a quarter turn. Repeat the process. Knead for around 10 minutes until the dough is smooth and satiny.

Rest the dough in a lightly oiled bowl some place warm, covered with a clean tea towel, until it has risen by half its original size. This should take around 45 minutes to 1 hour.

Preheat your oven to 200°C.

Once it's risen, tip the dough out onto a bench and knock all the air out with your fingertips, then roughly shape the dough into a loaf and place it in a lightly floured 25cm bread tin. Leave the dough to rise once more, this time for around 30 minutes, then lightly dust with flour and bake in the oven for 30 minutes.

When done the loaf should easily come out of the tin and sound hollow when tapped. If it doesn't sound drum-like and hollow, pop it back in the oven without the tin for another 10 minutes.

When it's cooked, leave it to cool to room temperature on a wire rack.

A light, fluffy bread roll is always welcome in my kitchen. They're the perfect vessel for cold meats, pickles and cheese, or to use as an edible sponge for rich, saucy braises. These buns are simple to make, with the fresh, full cream milk adding a little extra richness and a soft texture.

Milk Buns

MAKES 12

180ml (¾ cup) water

180ml (¾ cup) full cream milk

60ml (¼ cup) olive oil

Pinch of caster sugar

Pinch of salt

600g (4¾ cups) hard white bread flour

1 x 7g sachet dried yeast

In a small saucepan, gently heat the water, milk, oil, sugar and salt. Heat the mixture until it's warm to the touch, then remove from the heat.

In a mixing bowl combine the flour and yeast, and then pour the milk mixture in. Bring it all together with your hands until a dough is formed. Turn the dough out onto a lightly floured bench and gently knead it by pushing into the dough with the heels of your hands and then forward along the bench to stretch it. Fold the dough back on itself, rotate it a quarter turn and repeat. Knead for about 10 minutes until the dough is smooth and satiny.

Shape the dough into a big ball and place it in a lightly oiled bowl. Cover with a clean tea towel and place somewhere warm until the dough has doubled in size (about half an hour).

Turn the dough out onto a floured surface and knock the air out with your fingertips. Divide the dough into a dozen equal portions and shape into rolls. Place the rolls on a floured baking tray, cover with a clean tea towel and leave to prove for around 45 minutes or until doubled in size.

Preheat the oven to 220°C.

Once the buns have risen, slide the tray into the hot oven and bake for 15 minutes or until the tops are golden. Allow to cool slightly, then tear open and enjoy.

This simple, sweet-tasting, crumbly bread is about as easy as bread baking gets. There's minimal kneading and no proving. The resulting loaf is perfect when lightly toasted on a grill and served with offaly treats like parfait or seared liver.

Beer Bread

MAKES 1 LOAF

450g (3 cups) self-raising flour
Pinch of salt
375ml (1½ cups) golden ale, cold
75g butter, melted

Preheat the oven to 200°C and lightly butter and line a 20cm bread tin.

Sift the flour into a large mixing bowl. Pop in a pinch of salt, then make a well in the centre of the flour, pour in the cold beer and gently mix until the dough is evenly combined.

Pour the mixture into the prepared tin, then pour over the melted butter. Bake for 40 minutes. The loaf should have a beautiful golden crust and sound hollow when tapped.

Stand your bread on a wire rack and enjoy it while it's warm.

Of the few dishes that have achieved culinary canonisation as traditional Australian recipes, the one that most vividly conjures up images of the Outback and days gone by has to be damper. A simple soda bread, it was traditionally baked on the glowing coals of a campfire. Made from the most basic ingredients, damper fuelled many a swagman's wanderings over dusty country tracks. Damper can also be baked in a camp oven or even in a regular oven at home. I've replaced some of the water with buttermilk to enrich the flavour – I'm sure the old swaggies wouldn't mind a slight deviation from tradition.

Damper

MAKES 1 LARGE LOAF

900g (6 cups) self-raising flour, plus extra for dusting

Pinch of salt

750ml (3 cups) buttermilk (or plain full cream milk)

Water, as needed

If you're using a camp oven, build a fire and get a nice bed of coals going. If you're baking it in an oven at home, lightly grease a baking tray and preheat your oven to 200°C.

In a bowl combine the flour and salt, then make a well and pour in the buttermilk (or milk). Combine everything to form a smooth, slightly moist dough. If the dough feels a little dry slowly add water until you get the right feel. Shape the dough into a round loaf and lightly dust flour over the top before baking.

If you're using the camp oven, set the oven on a bed of gently glowing coals, place the loaf inside, put the lid on and, using a shovel, lay some coals over the camp oven. Bake for around 35 minutes or until the loaf has a golden crust and sounds hollow when tapped.

If you're baking your damper in a regular oven, place the loaf on a preheated oven tray and bake for 35–40 minutes. Again, you want the loaf to have a golden brown crust and sound hollow when tapped.

Serve with cultured butter (see page 240), golden syrup and hot cups of billy tea.

Making your own pizza dough is a great example of how a little kitchen wizardry can go a long way. A homemade dough equals automatic bragging rights as your family or guests gobble up slice after slice and still call for more. All it needs to elevate your culinary tricks to legendary status are a few simple toppings. Passata, mozzarella and basil is a classic, but feel free to experiment — just remember, when it comes to making a cracking pizza, less is more.

Pizza Dough

MAKES 3 BASES

375ml (1½ cups) warm water

1 x 7g sachet dried yeast

Pinch of caster sugar

600g (4¾ cups) hard white bread flour

60ml (¼ cup) olive oil

Pinch of salt

In a glass or small jug combine the water, yeast and sugar. Place somewhere nice and warm until the mixture starts to become foamy. Put the flour into a large mixing bowl. Add the yeasty water to the flour, along with the oil and salt. Using your hands mix it all together until a dough forms, then turn it out onto a floured bench and knead by pushing forward into the dough with the heels of your hands to stretch it. Fold the dough back on itself, rotate it a quarter turn and repeat until it becomes smooth and elastic (about 10 minutes).

Place the dough in a lightly oiled bowl, cover with a clean tea towel and set aside some place warm for about half an hour or until the dough has doubled in size.

Once doubled, turn the dough out onto your floured bench and use your fingertips or fists to knock the air out of the dough. I personally prefer the delicate approach with the fingertips, though I have seen plenty of people use their fists to vent some pent-up frustration on an unsuspecting pizza dough.

Divide the flattened dough into three equal portions and roll each one out into a base. I like my pizza bases nice and thin so I roll the dough out on a well-floured bench, lifting and turning as I go so that it doesn't stick.

TO COOK A PIZZA

A pizza oven is the best option, followed by a preheated pizza stone or a hot tray in a regular oven. Don't stress the details, though; all of the above will produce a top-notch pizza. Simply cover your rolled base with your desired toppings and then slide it into a very hot oven (250°C should do the trick). You'll know that the base is cooked by lifting up an edge of the pizza: if the bottom is dry and lightly browned, you're good to go.

Good bread and olive oil go hand in hand, so why not
combine the two and make a delicious focaccia bread?
It's so flavoursome that it can be enjoyed plain with
a little salt or used as a vessel for whatever toppings
your imagination can muster.

Focaccia

SERVES 6

450g (3½ cups) hard white bread flour

5g salt

5g dried yeast

About 300ml warm water

150ml extra-virgin olive oil, plus a little extra

Place the flour, salt and yeast into a large bowl, and then pour in the water. Bring the dough together and knead it in the bowl by pushing firmly into the dough with the heel of your hand, then folding and rotating it a quarter turn. Repeat this process, kneading for 5 minutes or until the dough is smooth yet soft, loose and sticky.

Add a good splash of olive oil to the dough and then knead it into the dough. Pour the remainder of the oil into the bowl and give the dough a good roll around to make sure that the dough is evenly coated. Cover the bowl with a clean tea towel and leave it at room temperature to prove for 2 hours or until the dough has doubled in size.

Brush a roasting tray generously with oil. Fold the outside edges of the dough into the centre, knocking the air out as you do so. Transfer the dough onto the oiled tray. Use your fingertips to push the dough down until it's about 2cm thick; the surface should be covered in indentations.

Now's the time to add toppings to the focaccia. It could be as simple as rosemary and salt, something a little more fancy like broad beans and spring garlic, or even a sweet topping such as pears and brown sugar. You're limited only by your imagination!

Brush the dough with more olive oil and leave to prove again for three-quarters of an hour or until the dough is light and risen.

Preheat the oven to 220°C and bake the focaccia for 10 minutes. Turn the tray by 180 degrees, reduce the oven temperature to 200°C and bake for a further 10 minutes or until the surface of the focaccia is nicely browned.

Remove from the oven and apply one last brush of olive oil. Let the focaccia cool a little and enjoy warm.

This thin Middle Eastern cracker adds a touch of homemade flair on a special cheese board, or if you prefer, you can serve it with dips or as a tasty appetiser. It's crunchy, salty and very difficult to stop eating.

Lavosh

MAKES ENOUGH FOR ABOUT 8 PEOPLE FOR NIBBLIES

185g plain flour

Small bunch of thyme, leaves picked

Pinch of salt

125ml (½ cup) extra-virgin olive oil

185ml (¾ cup) water

Poppy seeds

Salt flakes

Preheat your oven to 170°C.

Sift the flour into a large mixing bowl and add the thyme leaves and the salt. Make a well in the centre of the flour mix and pour in the oil and water, mixing with your hand as you go. Mix gently until you have a dough that is smooth, soft and pliable. It will be quite a wet dough.

Lay two sheets of baking paper on the bench and flour them lightly. Divide the dough into two, then roll out each portion on the paper until wafer-thin. Carefully transfer the two pieces of paper with the dough on them onto two baking trays.

Generously sprinkle the dough with poppy seeds and salt flakes. Slash the dough into rough strips. You can be as casual as you like with this step. I personally use a pizza cutter to cut lengths that are roughly 5cm across – they don't need to be perfect.

Bake in the oven for about 18 minutes or until crisp and lightly golden.

Remove from the oven and transfer the lavosh to a wire rack to cool. Once cool break up the strips into generously sized pieces.

You can make these in advance and they'll keep for a couple of days in an airtight container. The only problem is that they are such a delicious snack that if I prepare them in advance there are never any left when I need them.

DAIRY

Until I came to live at River Cottage Australia, milk was something that came in a plastic bottle from the supermarket. It was never anything to get particularly excited about; it was cheap and it was great in a cup of tea or for making porridge. It wasn't until I acquired my own house cow that I realised how much work goes into producing milk, and how good it can taste. I purchased a doe-eyed Jersey cow that had just given birth to a little bull calf from local dairy farmer Nic Dibden. My logic was that the cow, which I named Bessie in a stroke of creative genius, would produce enough milk for both the calf and myself and all that I would have to do is stroll up to the milking shed to fill my pail every morning. I planned to let the calf feed off his mother all day and then separate them of an evening, so that come morning, Bessie would have a full udder ready for me to milk.

The first morning I woke up just before sunrise, led Bessie into her stall, placed a shiny new pail under her udder and commenced milking – or should I say, trying to milk. I had never milked a cow before and the quick lesson that Nic had given me the day before was now a patchy memory. When he had shown me how it was done, the milk shot out of the teats like water from a high-pressure hose, hitting the bottom of the pail with a satisfying rhythm. My first attempt was not so awe inspiring, and after about 15 minutes Bessie was fed up with my incompetence and mooed a protest to be released. I had managed to fumble my way to a single paltry litre. That first litre didn't even make it back to the house. I lifted the pail to my mouth and drank the lot. I had never tasted anything like it – the milk was warm, rich and creamy, with a sweetness and a hint of grass. I was hooked. There was no way I could go back to the bottled stuff if this is what it tasted like straight from the cow. One thing was certain: I was going to have to get better at milking, and fast.

After a couple of weeks I got the hang of milking and was soon presented with a new problem. Every day Bessie was yielding anywhere between 5 and 20 litres of milk, depending on how successful the calf had been at getting a drink through the fence overnight. I had the stuff coming out of my ears, and no matter how much I drank or gave away to friends it kept coming and coming. However, I realised that milk is an incredibly versatile liquid that can be used for so much more than just something to put in your tea.

The milk that Bessie produced was rich in cream, and after letting the pail sit for a couple of hours a thick layer of creamy goodness would form on top. I had thought that the milk was good, but this cream was something else altogether. It was so thick and rich that it was practically butter; in fact, it only took a few seconds of whipping to turn it into the most vibrant yellow butter I had ever seen. I soon adopted the habit of putting aside a couple of litres for my friends and myself every day, taking the cream off the rest and feeding the leftover skim milk to the pigs. While this kept my pigs fat and happy, it still grated on me that I couldn't find something else to do with my excess milk. There had to be another solution.

Finding a way of preserving excess milk has been a challenge that's faced farmers since dairy animals were first domesticated. It turns out that the key to preserving milk products can be found in a most unlikely ally: bacteria. By harnessing these microscopic workers, milk can be turned into yoghurts and all manner of cheese. This transformation distills the fat, protein and calcium of milk into something that has a longer shelf life and is much easier to transport. I had to learn this ancient craft so that I could make the most of Bessie's bounty of milk. Fortunately for me, Central Tilba is home to a talented cheese maker named Erica, who has been incredibly helpful in sharing some of her cheesy wisdom and who also happens to be the wife of Nic the dairy farmer. I'm still on my cheese-making L plates, but much to the dismay of my pigs more and more of my milk is being diverted into things like yoghurt, fresh curd, ricotta and burrata.

Of course, cows are not the only farm animals that produce milk that is fit for human consumption. When I let Bessie's milk supply dry up in preparation for getting her pregnant again, I acquired two Saanen dairy goats to fill the void. Although a goat doesn't produce milk in the same abundance as a cow, it provides milk that is naturally lighter,

a little bit sweeter and has its own unique flavour. With a much lower butterfat content than cow's milk, goat's milk isn't ideally suited to cream and butter production but it can be used to make wonderful curd, cheeses and yoghurt.

Having your own cow or goat is not a prerequisite for making your own dairy goods. If you live in an area that produces milk, approach a local farmer and ask to buy milk directly from them. If that's not an option, seek out the highest quality fresh milk you can get your hands on from a supermarket or grocery store. It doesn't matter if the milk is pasteurised or homogenised, as long as it's not ultra pasteurised (UP) or ultra heat treated (UHT). When making any dairy product the fresher the milk is the better, so if you're buying it from a shop, make sure that the use-by date is still a while off. Once you discover how easy it is to make your own butter, yoghurt and simple cheeses, you'll never want to eat the store-bought stuff again.

'Cultured' butter isn't butter that has read a lot of classic Russian literature or that is well versed in the who's who of Post Impressionism. It's much more exciting than that – it's butter made from cream that has fermented ever so slightly to provide a delicious tang. If you're going to the effort of making your own butter then you need the best possible, high-fat, unadulterated cream that you can get your hands on. If you're lucky enough to have access to unpasteurised cream then there will be a host of friendly bacteria present to do the fermenting for you. Most likely, though, you'll have to settle for the store-bought stuff, which will benefit from the addition of some bacteria-dense natural yoghurt.

Cultured Butter

MAKES ABOUT 400G OF BUTTER FOR EACH LITRE OF CREAM

1 teaspoon natural yoghurt (see page 245) for each litre of cream

Pasteurised double cream (at least 1 litre), preferably Jersey

Iced water

1 teaspoon of salt for each litre of cream

Whisk 1 teaspoon of yoghurt into each litre of cream, and leave the cream in the fridge for up to 12 hours before churning. If you're using farm-fresh cream, leave it at room temperature for 24 hours before churning.

The next day, put the cream in a stand-mixer, and use the whisk attachment to churn it on medium speed. First the cream will whip and then you'll start to see little yellow globules of fat separating from the cream, and as if by magic the cream separates into butter and buttermilk. Pour the mixture into a colander to catch the butter, with a bowl set underneath to catch the buttermilk. Pour the buttermilk into a small jug and keep it in the fridge – you can use it later in place of milk for baking or as a tangy base for a salad dressing.

Pour some iced water over the butter in the colander, all the while turning it and kneading it, to rinse off the last of the buttermilk.

Transfer the butter to a clean chopping board and sprinkle over the salt. Knead the butter briefly to force out any excess liquid and to evenly distribute the salt. Shape the butter into a log, cut it into two pieces and wrap with baking paper. You can keep one in the fridge to use within a month, and put the other in the freezer, where it will keep for at least six months.

The intricacies of cheese making are still quite new to me. I'm yet to master any of the more advanced cheeses, such as Cheddars and gooey-centred washed rinds, but I can confidently say that I can make, with almost faultless consistency, the most basic of all cheeses, the humble curd. Requiring minimum patience, a pot, some milk and some vinegar, this training wheel of the cheese world is within everyone's grasp, and the creamy curd is a great foundation for many a culinary treat. You'll have some whey left over, but don't throw it away – it can be used for poaching meat, as a soup base or to make ricotta (see page 244).

Fresh Curd Cheese

MAKES ABOUT 200G

2 litres (8 cups) full cream cow's or goat's milk – the fresher the better

½ teaspoon salt

60ml (¼ cup) white vinegar

Pour the milk into a heavy-based saucepan along with the salt. Have a probe thermometer ready and gradually bring the temperature up to 80°C. As soon as the milk reaches this temperature, turn off the heat and add the vinegar, giving it the slightest stir to ensure that the vinegar is evenly dispersed. If you look carefully you can see the curds separating from the whey almost instantly.

Leave the vinegar to work its magic for 5 minutes, by which stage the curds and whey will be completely separated. Meanwhile, line a colander with a muslin cloth or clean tea towel. Use a slotted spoon to gently scoop the curds out of the pot into the colander, leaving the whey behind.

Now you have your curds you can mix through herbs and seasonings (like thyme and smoked paprika), add a little cream to make a cottage cheese, or keep the curd plain to use in things like sweet little curd cakes or a warm curd cake (see page 263).

Whenever I make a simple curd from fresh milk I'm left with loads of nutritious whey. What to do with left-over whey from cheese making has been a question since curds and whey first parted, well ... ways. In fact, whey has lots of uses, and my favourite of these is making ricotta. The process is pretty much the same as for making curds and whey. The yield isn't enormous, but the creamy, versatile ricotta more than justifies the effort.

Ricotta

MAKES ABOUT 100G

3 litres fresh whey, left over from making curds (see page 242)

1 teaspoon salt

30ml white wine vinegar

Pour the whey and salt into a large, heavy-based saucepan and, measuring with a probe thermometer, very gradually bring the temperature up to 88°C. Once the whey has reached this temperature, pour in the vinegar and give the pot one quick stir. Turn the heat off and leave the liquid for 10 minutes or so as the delicate ricotta curds separate. Meanwhile, line a colander with some fine muslin or a clean tea towel, and set it over the sink.

After the 10 minutes have passed, the curds will have separated and risen to the surface. Use a slotted spoon to very gently bring them to the centre of the pot to make them easier to collect.

Gently spoon them into the colander. Tie the muslin cloth into a pouch around the curd and leave it to hang for a couple of hours for the excess liquid to drain.

Delicately scoop the ricotta out of the cloth and store it in the fridge for up to a week.

Making yoghurt is simple and deeply satisfying. You need fresh milk, a small amount of a lively yoghurt to kick start the process, some heat and patience. And once you've made yourself a tub of this natural health food, you can use it as a tangy, cooling foil to a spicy curry or flavour it up with honey and berries for a sweet start to the day. Easy.

Natural Yoghurt

MAKES 1 LITRE

1 litre (4 cups) full cream cow's or goat's milk, the best that you can get your hands on

125ml (½ cup) store-bought natural yoghurt, made from cow's or goat's milk – again, get the good stuff and make sure that it contains live cultures

A good probe thermometer comes in handy for this recipe, though if you don't have one you can estimate with your eye and by touch.

Pour the milk into a heavy-based saucepan and gradually bring the heat up to 85°C – this is the point just below the boil, when the surface starts to steam. Once this temperature has been reached, remove the pot from the heat and let the milk cool to 45°C or slightly warmer than room temperature. You can speed up this process by setting the pot into a sink filled with cold water.

Once the milk has cooled sufficiently, take a ladleful and whisk it into the 125ml yoghurt, then pour the thinned yoghurt back into the milk. The milk is now ready to ferment into yoghurt – all it needs is a little time and a nice, warm place to sit.

Cover the pot with a lid or tea towel and set on a mantle piece above the fire or in an oven with the pilot light on. Let it sit for around 8–10 hours. I like to make mine in the evening and let it stand overnight.

Come the morning, the cultures will have turned the milk into a big wobbly pot of yoghurt. Transfer the yoghurt into a container and then refrigerate to thicken further. This yoghurt will keep in the fridge for a fortnight; just make sure that you keep half a cup for next time.

If you like making your own yoghurt then you should definitely try your hand at making labne. This tangy strained yoghurt – like a soft, fresh cheese – can be added to green beans to give them a creamy, sour kick (see page 54), used in a side salad to offset the heat of pepperberry-crusted venison (see page 167) or coupled with bacon in an omelette for a tasty brekkie (see page 197).

Labne

MAKES ABOUT 500ML

1 litre (4 cups) natural yoghurt, made from full cream cow's or goat's milk (see page 245)

A good pinch of salt

Line a colander with muslin and set it over a pot or bowl – anything will work really, as long as there is room for the liquid to drain off the yoghurt.

Mix the salt and yoghurt together and spoon it onto the muslin cloth, then fold the muslin over it to cover.

Put it in the fridge and let it stand for 12 hours for a creamy, thick labne or leave it for 24 hours for a more firm labne that can be rolled into balls and then stored in olive oil.

I can barely speak a word of Italian but I'm pretty sure that burrata translates to delicious, cheesy, cream bomb. Basically a ball of mozzarella stuffed with cream, burrata may take a bit of effort, a few weird ingredients and some burnt fingers, but believe me, the results are worth it. The weird ingredients (the calcium chloride and rennet) are essential for helping the curd separate and set, and are easily acquired through cheese-making sites on the internet. The leftover whey can be used for enriching bread dough, braising meats or fattening pigs.

Burrata

MAKES 4 BURRATA

4 litres unhomogenised full cream milk

2ml calcium chloride (omit if using raw/unpasteurised milk)

2 teaspoons citric acid dissolved in 60ml (¼ cup) cold water

¼ teaspoon liquid vegetable rennet, diluted in 60ml (¼ cup) water

125ml (½ cup) pure cream

Salt

Pour the milk and the calcium chloride (if using) into a heavy-based, stainless steel pot and gently heat it until a probe thermometer reads 13°C. Add the citric acid mixture and gently stir while steadily bringing the temperature up until the thermometer reads 32°C. Once that temperature has been reached, remove the pot from the heat and add the rennet mixture, stirring it through by using an up and down motion with a spoon, trying not to disturb the forming curd. Cover the pot and let it sit for 30 minutes while the curds coagulate.

When the curds are at a stage where they pull away from the side of the pot, use a long knife to cut the curd into a grid of 4cm squares, being certain that the curd has been cut all the way from top to bottom. Return the pot to the heat and gently bring the temperature up to a reading of around 45°C on the thermometer. Remove from the heat once more and slowly and gently stir the curds for a couple of minutes – this helps the curds to firm a little.

Ladle the curds into a colander that's been lined with muslin cloth or a clean tea towel and set over a bowl in the sink. Allow to drain, reserving the whey for another use. Transfer a quarter of the curds to a separate bowl and break apart into little chunks. Stir through the cream and a pinch of salt to achieve a consistency like runny cottage cheese. This will be the filling for the burrata.

Fill a medium-sized bowl with iced water.

Set out a bowl that's large enough to hold the colander full of curds. Fill the bowl with boiling water and then very gently ease the colander in. Put on rubber gloves and as soon as you can handle it, separate the curd into 4 balls and then proceed to stretch and work each one, folding the cheese back on itself until it has become smooth and glossy. This should take around 5 minutes for each ball. The water needs to be almost

unbearably hot, so have a kettle handy as you may have to change the water in the bowl to keep it at the right temperature.

Once the curd is smooth and glossy, stretch the first ball out to form a flat disc just under 1cm thick. Onto this disc, spoon a big dollop of the cream-and-curd mixture, fold the disc up to form a little pouch, and then firmly pinch the edges to seal. The burrata should resemble a little bomb or a poached egg. Once the burrata has been sealed, pop it in the bowl of iced water to set and repeat with the remaining three balls.

Eat these tasty cream bombs on the day that they're made for the best results. I like mine with roasted beetroot and garden greens on a slice of toasted rye bread (see page 223). Delicious.

SWEET THINGS

I have a sweet tooth. There is no point in denying it or being ashamed of it – I love all things that tickle the certain part of my tongue that detects sweetness. I know that I inherited this trait from my father, who hasn't baked a cake in his life but can always be relied on to have a secret stash of chocolate tucked away in the pantry. If it was my Dad who instilled in me the need for the odd sweet treat, then it was definitely my grandmother who supplied the goods. When I was a kid she would babysit us on the school holidays and spend a good chunk of the day in the kitchen turning out all manner of drool-inducing wonders. She was an old-school country cook, so jam drops, sponges and chocolate cakes were all welcome staples. At the time I had absolutely no interest in the process – there was too much going on outside to be cooped up in a kitchen – but when the time came to clean the chocolate out of a bowl or help take a tray of biscuits out of the oven I had an uncanny knack of being present. As an adult I had to learn to fend for myself in the kitchen and now find great joy in whipping together a simple dessert or a cake to take to a friend's house. The pleasure lies in the alchemy of turning humble ingredients – sugar, butter, eggs and flour – into something magnificent. There are few things in this world that fill me with more delight than a slice of moist chocolate cake that's still warm from the oven, served with a scoop of fragrant vanilla ice cream.

Churning out quality baked goods has long been a part of the social fabric of this country. They are a token of hospitality when friends visit, a way of raising money for small communities and a little pick-me-up for someone who's under the weather. They're the food that we turn to when we're feeling down and want a small ray of delicious hope. Sure, these treats aren't essential to our survival, but could you imagine a world without ice cream, doughnuts or honeycomb? No smoko break would be complete without a cuppa and a homemade bikkie. Christmas just wouldn't be the same without an enormous pavlova, slathered in rich cream and topped with a dazzling array of summer fruits. Although I'm not saying that we should be eating cake for breakfast, lunch and dinner (not most days, anyway), I can't help but feel that life is made that little bit more awesome when you can enjoy something that's not good for the waistline but good for the soul.

Making a simple dessert or a tray of baked goods doesn't have to be an elaborate affair. In fact, with only a few staples in the pantry and fridge there's no limit to the wonderful cakes, biscuits and desserts that you can whip up in a flash.

SUGAR

We're lucky enough to have climate regions in Australia that are suitable for sugar cane production, and we grow millions of tonnes of the stuff every year. There is a dazzling array of sugar products available to us as consumers but there is only a small handful that I would bother keeping stocked in the pantry. If you only want to stock one type, make it caster sugar. This super-fine workhorse can be used in everything from cakes to caramel. In addition to caster sugar, I keep a little pure icing sugar for icing the odd chockie cake and making my sweet shortcrust pastry.

VANILLA BEANS

There is something uniquely intoxicating about a fresh vanilla bean that no extract or substitute can match, so I always like to keep a couple stashed in the pantry. As there is only a fledgling Australian vanilla-growing industry, domestically grown beans can be difficult to source and the bulk of vanilla beans available here are imported. If you're buying imported beans, be sure that they are covered by a fair trade agreement so that a good chunk of the money goes back into the pocket of the farmer who grew them. To store your beans, pop them in a brown paper bag and place it in a dark corner of the pantry. The key is to not let the beans dry out; beans stored this way should last for up to six months. To get maximum economy from your vanilla beans, after you've scraped the seeds out store the skins in a jar of sugar or in a carton of eggs to infuse with the pungent vanilla aroma.

FLOUR

A quality, unbleached plain white flour will do the job for the bulk of your baking needs. With a protein content of around 7% to 10% it's soft enough to make cakes but strong enough to make biscuits and pie crusts. If you keep a little baking powder in the pantry you can also make your own self-raising flour using 3g of baking powder for every 100g of plain flour.

DARK CHOCOLATE

I always have a couple of blocks of good quality dark chocolate in the pantry. I prefer eating chocolate with 70% cocoa content for a few reasons. The first is that even though eating chocolate is a little more expensive than cooking chocolate, it has a much better flavour. Second, dark chocolate has a richer, more complex flavour than milk chocolate, which will give you a better-tasting end result. Finally, if you don't want to bake anything you can just eat the chocolate by itself!

BUTTER

I always keep a decent lump of unsalted butter in the fridge. Delicious food is made with quality ingredients so look for the best stuff that you can get your hands on.

CREAM

Good quality double cream will serve you well for all your baking purposes. It has a high fat content that's ideal for making rich custards, and when whipped it's a staple garnish to dollop on top of pavlovas, warm cakes, puddings and sweet pies.

EGGS

In a perfect world, we'd all be able to keep a couple of chooks to provide us with a steady supply of golden-yolked eggs. If you don't have your own chickens, then seek out eggs from birds that live their lives outdoors, on pasture. If purchasing your eggs in the supermarket, make sure that any claims of 'free range' are certified by an independent body and that the birds are stocked at a rate of 1500 per hectare or less.

When I was a little tacker my Nan would whip up the most unbelievable chocolate cake. Once she started mixing, I would circle her like an annoying little blowfly, hoping for a lick of a beater, a surplus piece of chocolate or the ultimate – the whole mixing bowl to lick clean.

Nan's no longer with us but every time I open the oven door and get a waft of this cake cooking I know she's not far away. This one's for you, Nan.

Nanna Guy's Murrurundi Mountain Mud Cake

SERVES 10

225g (1½ cups) plain flour

150g (1 cup) self-raising flour

30g (¼ cup) cocoa

250g unsalted butter, roughly chopped

200g high-quality dark chocolate, roughly chopped

2 free-range eggs

460g (2 cups) caster sugar

250ml (1 cup) full cream milk

½ teaspoon salt

ICING

50g dark cooking chocolate

300g unsalted butter, softened

40g cocoa

100g pure icing sugar, sifted

40ml full cream milk

Cocoa, for dusting

Preheat the oven to 160°C and then grease and line a 23cm round springform cake tin.

Sift the plain flour, self-raising flour and cocoa together.

Combine the butter and chocolate in a bowl that will sit comfortably on a pot of gently simmering water. (Make sure the water doesn't touch the bottom of the bowl.) Leave the bowl over the pot, stirring occasionally, until the butter and chocolate have melted.

In a large mixing bowl, whisk together the eggs and sugar until they are smooth and light. Pour in the milk and continue mixing until everything is evenly combined.

Sift the flour/cocoa mix *again* into the egg/milk mix, then gently fold in until you have a smooth batter. Next, fold through the melted chocolate and butter (keep the empty bowl to one side as you can reuse it for the icing), along with the ½ teaspoon of salt.

Pour the mixture into the cake tin and let it all rest in the fridge for 10 minutes or so.

Once rested, place the cake tin in the oven and bake for 45–50 minutes, giving it a turn around halfway through. The cake is ready when an inserted skewer comes out dotted with a few moist crumbs.

Let the cake stand for a few minutes, then transfer from the tin to a cooling rack.

While the cake is cooling you can make the icing. Using the same bowl as before, melt the chocolate over simmering water. In a separate mixing bowl, use an electric beater to whisk together the butter, cocoa and icing sugar until smooth. Slowly add the milk, then the melted chocolate. Beat it all together until the mix is smooth and fluffy.

Once the cake is cool, spread the icing evenly on top. For a final touch, Nan used to give the whole thing a light dusting of cocoa.

The polar oppposite of an airy sponge, this dense,
nutty cake is kept moist and given a lift by the addition
of the orange syrup. A great cake recipe to have up
your sleeve for those among us who avoid the wheatier
things in life.

Hazelnut Syrup Cake

SERVES 12

6 free-range eggs, separated

150g caster sugar

2 teaspoons baking powder

Zest of 2 oranges

**340g hazelnuts, ground to
a fine meal**

**Candied peel, to serve
(optional)**

ORANGE SYRUP

150g caster sugar

**200ml freshly squeezed
orange juice**

Zest of 4 oranges

Preheat the oven to 160°C and grease and line a 25cm cake tin.

In a large mixing bowl, use an electric whisk to beat together
the egg yolks and sugar until they are creamy and pale yellow.

In a separate bowl, mix together the baking powder, orange zest
and hazelnut meal, then add to the egg yolks and sugar and
thoroughly beat them together.

In a clean bowl whisk the egg whites until stiff peaks form.
Add one-third of the whisked whites to the yolk mixture and
combine to help lighten the mixture, then gently fold in the
remaining whites until the mixture has a smooth, even consistency.
Pour the batter into the prepared cake tin and bake for about an
hour or until the cake springs back lightly when touched and
a skewer inserted into the centre of the cake comes out clean.

While the cake is cooking, make the syrup. Combine all the
ingredients in a saucepan and stir over a medium heat. Once
the sugar is dissolved reduce the heat and simmer for 2 minutes.
Allow to cool.

When the cake is cooked, remove from the tin and while it is
still hot, prick it all over with a skewer and then spoon half of
the syrup on top, allowing it to soak in. Leave to cool a little.

To serve, dress with more syrup and some candied peel, if
you like.

Lemon tart is one of my all-time favourite desserts. The crumble of the pastry, the slightly tart lemon, the velvety curd – it really is an amazing balance of textures and flavours. Aussie grown lemons are available year round, so this tarty treat can be enjoyed any time. You can substitute a store-bought tart case for the homemade pastry.

Lemon Tart

SERVES 8

PASTRY

300g (2 cups) plain flour

150g unsalted butter, cold, roughly cut into 1 cm cubes

½ teaspoon salt

120g (1 cup) pure icing sugar, plus extra for dusting

3 large free-range egg yolks, whisked

FILLING

5 lemons – juice of 5, zest of 2

300ml double cream

400g caster sugar

10 free-range eggs

Using the paddle attachment of a stand-mixer combine the flour, butter and salt until the texture resembles coarse sand or fine breadcrumbs. If you don't have an electric mixer you can massage the butter and flour together, rubbing it between your fingertips until a sandy/breadcrumb texture is achieved.

In a separate bowl, combine the icing sugar and egg yolks and then add to the flour mix. Combine until a moist dough forms. Turn the dough out onto a lightly floured bench and mould into a flat circle that resembles a smaller version of the tart tin that you intend to bake with. Rest the pastry in the fridge for an hour.

When the pastry is ready, roll it out onto a lightly floured bench to a thickness of around 3mm. Gently roll the pastry up around the rolling pin and then unroll it over a lightly greased 25cm tart tin, being sure to leave plenty of pastry hanging over the sides. Using the tips of your fingers gently press in around all the corners. Prick the surface of the pastry all over with a fork and leave to rest in the fridge again for half an hour.

Preheat the oven to 190°C.

Once the pastry has rested, remove it from the fridge. Line it with baking paper and weigh the paper with rice, beans or blind-baking weights and bake for 20 minutes. Remove the paper and weights and return the shell to the oven for another 5 minutes. The pastry should be dry to touch and slightly golden in colour. Remove from the oven and allow to cool.

Turn the oven down to 120°C.

To make the filling, combine all the ingredients in a stainless steel bowl and then place over a gently simmering pot of water. Gently stir the mixture until it reaches 60°C (it should just be starting to steam). Strain through a fine mesh strainer into a jug.

If you can, slide out an oven shelf and place the tart shell on it, pour the curd mix into the shell, filling it all the way to the rim and then gently, gently slide the oven shelf back in. If you can't slide out a shelf, fill the tart as close to the oven as possible – it takes a steady hand to get an unbaked lemon tart safely into the oven! Bake for 20 minutes or until set. Allow to cool and trim off the excess pastry. Dust with icing sugar right before serving.

This baked, baseless cheesecake is as simple as whizzing together all the ingredients and popping it in the oven for an hour. The curd provides a creamy texture and a pleasant tang that is perfectly accompanied by a big spoonful of tart, baked rhubarb.

Warm Curd Cake with Honey Rhubarb

SERVES 8

CURD CAKE

1kg fresh curd (see page 242)

230g (1 cup) caster sugar

115ml (½ cup) double cream

4 free-range eggs

Zest of 1 lemon

HONEY RHUBARB

½ bunch of rhubarb, ends trimmed, cut into short lengths

Juice and zest of 1 orange

2 tablespoons runny honey

Preheat your oven to 180°C and grease and line a 25cm cake tin.

Place the curd, sugar, cream, eggs and lemon zest in the bowl of a stand-mixer and whisk until everything is smooth and silky. If you don't have a mixer you can whisk it by hand – it'll just take a little more elbow grease.

Pour the batter into the prepared cake tin and smooth out any lumps and bumps with a spatula or the back of a spoon. Pop it in the oven and bake for 1 hour or until golden and set.

While the curd cake is baking, put the rhubarb pieces in a single layer in an ovenproof dish and scatter over the orange juice and zest. Trickle over the honey and mix so that the rhubarb is evenly coated. Place it in the oven alongside the cake and bake until soft and aromatic. That will be around 15–20 minutes.

To serve, allow the cake to cool a little, then slice and serve with a saucy spoonful of the honey rhubarb.

It's a bit of a tradition in the bush that whenever you head over to someone's house for a cuppa and a catch-up, you don't go empty-handed. There's no need for lavish gifts, just a simple cake or some bikkies will do the trick, and simple cakes don't get much easier than a pound cake.

This staple of the cake world takes its name from the weight needed for each of the four key ingredients: eggs, sugar, flour and butter. Although we dropped the imperial system of measurement decades ago, a 450g cake just doesn't have the same ring to it. For this recipe I've scaled back the weight a bit, and all the measurements are metric, but the same principle of equal weight of the four key ingredients stays true.

Lightly Spiced Pound Cake

SERVES 6

250g unsalted butter, softened

250g caster sugar

1 teaspoon vanilla extract

4 free-range eggs

250g plain flour

Zest of 1 lemon

2 teaspoons ground cardamom

Pure icing sugar, for dusting

Pure cream, whipped to soft peaks, to serve

Preheat your oven to 170°C and grease a 23cm loaf tin.

In a mixing bowl, beat together the softened butter, sugar and vanilla extract until pale and creamy. Scrape down the sides of the bowl and add 1 egg at a time, beating well until they are combined.

Sift the flour into the cake mixture, then add the lemon zest and ground cardamom and use a spatula to gently fold everything together.

Spoon the mixture into the prepared loaf tin and bake in the oven for about 50 minutes. The cake is done when a skewer inserted in the centre comes out clean.

Let the cake stand for 10 minutes, then remove from the tin. To serve, dust with icing sugar, cut into thick slices and garnish with a generous dollop of lightly whipped cream.

During my first summer at River Cottage Australia, I got a little carried away and planted two whole rows of zucchini. I realised my mistake when at the peak of their production I was harvesting a basket of zucchini every single day. The upside of this glut was that it inspired me to come up with new ways of using this plentiful ingredient. One of my more successful results is this delicious zucchini cake. The zucchini works brilliantly with a bit of tang from some lemon and a creamy mascarpone filling. Plus it's cake and vegetables combined, which makes it healthy, right?

Double-decker Zucchini Cake

SERVES 8

180g unsalted butter

180g (¾ cup) caster sugar

Juice and zest of 1 lemon

3 free-range eggs

100g self-raising flour

100g plain wholemeal flour

1½ teaspoons baking powder

1 teaspoon ground mixed spice

½ teaspoon salt

1 teaspoon poppy seeds

2 smallish zucchini

MASCARPONE FILLING

300ml double cream

250ml (1 cup) mascarpone

ICING

Zest and juice of 1 lemon

250g (2 cups) pure icing sugar

1 teaspoon poppy seeds

Preheat your oven to 180°C and grease and line 2 x 20cm round sandwich cake tins.

Place the butter, sugar and lemon zest in a large mixing bowl and whisk until pale and creamy. Add the eggs one by one and continue beating until well combined.

Sift the flours, baking powder, mixed spice and salt into a mixing bowl, then add the poppy seeds and give the bowl a toss to combine. Fold the flour and spices into the butter mixture until well combined.

Coarsely grate the zucchini into a colander and then press them against the sides of the colander to force out any excess moisture. Fold the zucchini and lemon juice into the cake batter and then divide it evenly between the prepared tins. Pop the tins into the oven and bake for 20–25 minutes, or until a skewer inserted in the middle comes out clean. Let the cakes cool for 5–10 minutes in the tins, then transfer to a wire rack to cool completely.

To make the mascarpone filling, whip the cream until it forms soft peaks. In a separate bowl beat the mascarpone to soften and then fold in the whipped cream. Set it aside while you make the icing.

To make the icing, combine the lemon juice and icing sugar in a medium-sized bowl and beat together well. The consistency should be thick but still the tiniest bit runny. If it's too thick, add a little more lemon juice or water. If it's too runny, add more icing sugar.

When the cake is completely cool, use a spatula to spread the creamy filling onto the top of one of the cakes. Next, gently place the other cake on top and spoon the icing on top of that, using a small spatula to make sure that the surface is evenly covered. Sprinkle over the poppy seeds and lemon zest and allow the icing to set.

Slice to serve and enjoy with a cuppa.

Shot into the limelight by a former first lady of Queensland, these delicious scones are a great smoko treat on a brisk, autumn morning. Some people hold that a secret blend of different pumpkins is the key to the perfect scone, but personally I find that straight butternut gives the best results.

Pumpkin Scones

MAKES **12** SCONES

350g butternut pumpkin, cut into small cubes

300g (2 cups) self-raising flour

1 teaspoon salt

40g unsalted butter, at room temperature

40g (⅓ cup) pure icing sugar

1 free-range egg

Full cream milk, for glazing (and a little extra if needed)

Cultured butter (see page 240) and honey, to serve

Preheat your oven to 180°C.

Use a colander over a pot of boiling water, or a vegetable steamer, to steam the pumpkin. Once the pumpkin is soft, arrange it on a tray lined with baking paper and quickly pop it in the oven to bake off any excess moisture. This should take around 10 minutes. Once the pumpkin is sufficiently dried, transfer it to a mixing bowl and mash it until it's smooth. Cover it up and pop it in the fridge to cool completely. No shortcuts here – if the pumpkin isn't totally cooled before being incorporated into the scone mix then the dough will be loose and sloppy!

Sift the flour into a clean mixing bowl, then add the salt and toss to combine evenly.

In a separate bowl, beat together the butter and icing sugar until it becomes pale and fluffy, then add the egg and continue beating until it's well incorporated. Next, beat in the cold, mashed pumpkin. Finally, add the flour and mix gently by hand to form a rough dough. If it's looking a little dry you can add a splash of milk to help bring it together.

Preheat your oven to 200°C.

Turn the dough out onto a very lightly floured surface and gently knead it by pushing into the dough with the heels of your hands to stretch it. Fold the dough back on itself, rotate it a quarter turn and repeat. Knead for about 5 minutes or until the dough becomes smooth. It should be the tiniest bit sticky to the touch but definitely not wet.

Roll the dough out to a thickness of 2cm and then use a 5cm cutter to cut it into rounds. Dip the cutter in flour so it doesn't stick. Transfer the rounds to a tray lined with baking paper, making sure that they are well spaced. Evenly brush the tops with a little milk and bake for 10–15 minutes or until risen and golden.

Once cooked, immediately transfer to a basket lined with a tea towel, then fold over the tea towel and allow them to sit for 10 minutes. To serve, twist the scones in half and cover with lashings of cultured butter and honey.

I grew up on my grandmother's jam drops. She'd bake them on the school holidays when she used to look after my sister and me. Unfortunately they seem to have fallen out of favour, though I can't for the life of me understand why. I'd take one of these chewy, berry jam–filled bikkies over a fancy macaron any day. Bring back the jam drops!

Jam Drops

MAKES AROUND 20 BIKKIES

125g unsalted butter, at room temperature

110g (½ cup) caster sugar

1 free-range egg

185g (1¼ cups) self-raising flour, sifted

60g (1 cup) desiccated coconut

Strawberry or rhubarb jam (see page 301)

Preheat your oven to 180°C and line two oven trays with baking paper.

In a mixing bowl, beat the butter and sugar until pale and creamy, then add the egg and continue beating until well combined. Add the sifted flour and desiccated coconut, and then stir gently until combined.

Use a tablespoon to scoop up a bit of dough, then roll it into a ball using your hands and place it on one of the baking trays. Repeat with the remaining dough.

Use the spoon to flatten the balls a little and then make an indentation with the tip of your pinky finger. Spoon some jam into the indentation and then place the trays in the oven to bake for 15 minutes or until golden.

Remove from the oven and spoon a little more jam into the indentations while the biscuits are still hot. Leave to stand for a couple of minutes on the baking trays and then transfer to a wire rack to cool completely.

Freshly made doughnuts are the business. Warm and fluffy with a sweet, crunchy, cinnamon coating, they make the perfect companion to a cup of strong black coffee.

Drop Doughnuts

SERVES 4

4 litres rice bran oil (or similar), for deep-frying

300g (2 cups) plain flour

110g (½ cup) caster sugar

3 teaspoons baking powder

½ teaspoon salt

125ml (½ cup) full cream milk

60g (¼ cup) unsalted butter, melted

2 free-range eggs

CINNAMON SUGAR

115g (½ cup) caster sugar

2 teaspoons ground cinnamon

Put a large, heavy-based saucepan on the stove and fill it with the frying oil. Heat the oil to 180°C.

Meanwhile, sift the flour into a mixing bowl and combine with the sugar, baking powder and the ½ teaspoon of salt.

In a separate bowl, whisk together the milk, melted butter and eggs. Pour the liquid ingredients over the dry ingredients and gently whisk together until a smooth batter has formed.

To check if the oil is hot enough, spoon a tiny amount of batter into the saucepan – if the batter bubbles up straight away you're good to go. Once the oil is up to temperature, use one tablespoon to scoop up some batter and use another to push it off into the oil. Repeat until there are a few doughnuts bobbing away happily in oil. When they are golden, lift out with a slotted spoon and place on some paper towel to soak up any excess oil. Be patient and don't overcrowd the pan – work in batches until all the batter is gone.

In a mixing bowl toss the sugar and ground cinnamon together. Drop the still-hot doughnuts into the sugar mix and roll them to ensure they're evenly coated. Enjoy them while they're warm.

I don't know who's happier when I make these crunchy, airy treats, my dentist or me. In spite of its name, honeycomb is often made without any honey at all. I've included it here, along with golden syrup and sugar, to add depth to the flavour. It's easy and even fun to make, as long as you get the temperature of the caramel just right – underdo it and the honeycomb will be chewy, overdo it and you'll have a smoking pot of burnt sugar. My favourite part is adding the bicarb soda, which seems part science, part magic – watch in awe as the caramel rapidly transforms into a puffy, golden cloud of honeycomb.

Honeycomb

MAKES ABOUT 20 PIECES

345g (1½ cups) caster sugar

115g (⅓ cup) honey

115g (⅓ cup) golden syrup

80ml (⅓ cup) water

2 teaspoons bicarbonate of soda

250g high-quality dark chocolate, roughly chopped

Place a large, deep-sided oven tray that has been completely lined with baking paper next to the stove.

Combine the caster sugar, honey, golden syrup and water in a large, deep-sided, heavy-based saucepan. Make sure the pan is a lot bigger than is required to hold the ingredients because once you add the bicarb soda all that hot, bubbling caramel will double in size. Heat the mix over a low heat, stirring occasionally until the sugar has dissolved.

Now, take a wet pastry brush and brush down any sugar crystals from the sides of the pot, then turn up the heat and don't stir until the caramel has almost reached the hard-crack stage. To check, you can use a sugar thermometer and wait until it reaches just under 150°C. Or you can drop a little caramel into a glass of water – if it solidifies into shards that can be easily cracked, it's ready.

Remove the pot from the heat and let the bubbling caramel calm down for a second, then add the bicarb soda, stirring vigorously with a spatula or wooden spoon to ensure that it's evenly mixed. Stand back and watch the caramel volcano show, then transfer the airy, golden mass to the lined tray and leave the honeycomb to cool completely.

While the honeycomb cools, melt the chocolate in a mixing bowl that is set over a pot of gently simmering water. Smash the honeycomb into bite-sized shards and then dip them in the melted chocolate. Set them on a rack and leave the chocolate to set. Enjoy the choc-coated chunks, or for an indulgent dessert smash the pieces even more and sprinkle over chocolate ice cream.

If you've got a little left over, store it in an airtight container somewhere cool and dry where it will keep for a week.

Christmas lunch just wouldn't be complete without
a top button–popping slice of pavlova. The gooey
meringue, with its crunchy crust, makes the perfect
base for generous lashings of whipped cream and
a medley of summer fruits. Both sides of the Tasman
loudly claim it as their national dish, but the one thing
that most Aussies and Kiwis *do* agree on is that pavlova
is way too good to be enjoyed only at Christmas.

Summer Pavlova

SERVES 6

4 free-range egg whites

½ teaspoon salt

1 vanilla pod, split, seeds scraped

250g caster sugar

TOPPING

250ml (1 cup) pure cream, whipped to stiff peaks

1 mango, peeled and cut into small pieces

2 freestone peaches, cut into small slices

Handful of strawberries, hulled and cut in half

Handful of blueberries

4 passionfruit

Preheat your oven to 150°C and line an oven tray with baking paper.

Combine the egg whites and salt together in a very clean, dry mixing bowl and then whisk until the whites form soft peaks.

Add the vanilla seeds to the egg whites and continue whisking while gradually adding the sugar. Keep whisking until the egg whites are voluminous, glossy and form stiff peaks when the whisk is removed.

Spoon the whisked whites into the centre of the lined baking tray. Using a spatula spread the meringue mix out to a diameter of around 20cm, then use the spatula to raise the meringue a little higher around the edges, making a shallow bowl shape.

Pop the tray in the oven and bake for around 1 hour. The meringue should have formed a crust but not coloured. Turn the oven off and allow the meringue to cool completely in the oven with the door ajar.

To serve, cover the top of the meringue with the whipped cream using a spatula. Scatter the mango, peaches, strawberries and blueberries over the cream. To finish, cut the passionfruit in half and scoop out the pulp and seeds over the top. Cut the pavlova into hearty slices and enjoy!

This rich, vanilla-flavoured cream is the perfect counterpoint to fresh, sweet summer berries. The cream and milk are set with just enough gelatine to hold their shape but as soon as you put a spoonful in your mouth it dissolves into creamy goodness. I don't worry about using individual moulds and turning them out – I find one big bowl and a couple of spoons does the job just fine.

Berry Panna Cotta

SERVES 4

2 gelatine leaves

300ml double cream

100ml full cream milk

20g caster sugar

1 vanilla pod, split, seeds scraped

SUMMER BERRIES

Small handful of strawberries, hulled, cut into chunky pieces

Small handful of raspberries

1 tablespoon pure icing sugar

A splash of water

Put the strawberry pieces and the raspberries in a small pot with the icing sugar and a splash of water. Cook over a low heat until the sugar has dissolved and the fruit has softened. Pour the berries into the bottom of a large, shallow serving bowl and then pop it in the fridge to cool.

Soak the gelatine leaves in cold water.

Pour the cream and milk into a pot, add the sugar and the vanilla pod and seeds and gently bring to a simmer.

Take the gelatine leaves and squeeze out any excess moisture, then add them to the cream mixture, remove the pot from the heat and stir to dissolve.

Strain the mixture into a cold jug and then gently pour it over the berries in the serving bowl. Place the bowl back in the fridge and allow the panna cotta to set. This will take a couple of hours. To tell if it's ready take the bowl out and give it a wobble – if the panna cotta moves like jelly it's ready to go.

This classic French dessert is traditionally made with black cherries, though you can enjoy it year round with any number of fruits. My favourite is made using ripe blackberries towards the end of summer. The juice-packed fruit burst through the batter as the clafoutis cooks, giving it a beautiful appearance that is matched by the lightness of the batter and the sweet, sharp flavour of the berries.

Blackberry Clafoutis

SERVES 6

100g (⅔ cup) plain flour, plus extra for dusting

50g (¼ cup) brown sugar

55g (¼ cup) caster sugar

2 free-range eggs

250ml (1 cup) pure cream, plus extra as needed

2 teaspoons vanilla extract

A little butter for greasing

300g (3½ cups) fresh blackberries

Pure icing sugar, for dusting

In a mixing bowl, combine the flour and sugars. In another small bowl, combine the eggs, cream and vanilla extract and whisk well. Make a well in the centre of the flour mixture and pour in the cream mixture in a steady, thin stream.

Whisk together to form a smooth batter. The consistency should be similar to a pancake batter – if it's a little firm add a touch more cream to loosen it up. Let it rest for 20–30 minutes.

Preheat the oven to 200°C. Butter and lightly flour a shallow 20cm baking dish (8-cup capacity).

Pour the batter into the prepared baking dish, scatter over the blackberries and press some into the batter. Bake for 25–30 minutes, or until golden and risen. Sprinkle over a little icing sugar and serve immediately.

This upside-down tart with its saucy caramel, gooey banana and flaky puff pastry is a sure-fire crowd pleaser. It's desserts like this that make a few pieces of puff pastry a staple in my freezer. One word of caution, though: as friendly as caramel is to the taste buds, don't mess around with it while it's hot – get burnt once and you'll never forget it.

Banana Tarte Tatin

SERVES 4

70g unsalted butter

140g caster sugar

5 firm bananas

1 sheet of frozen puff pastry, thawed

Vanilla bean ice cream (see page 294), to serve

Preheat your oven to 200°C.

Place a 25cm ovenproof frypan over a medium heat and then add the butter. Once the butter starts to melt and foam, stir in the sugar and continue cooking until it becomes a golden caramel colour, then remove the pan from the heat.

Peel the bananas and cut them in half lengthways. Snugly arrange the pieces in the pan, on top of the caramel.

Trim the pastry sheet, if necessary, so that it covers the pan with a little bit of overhang.

Lay the pastry over the banana-filled pan and tuck under the edges. Use the tip of a small knife to poke a few holes in the pastry and then pop the pan in the oven. Bake the tart for around 20 minutes or until the pastry is golden and puffed.

When it is cooked, remove from the oven and leave it to sit for a couple of minutes. Now comes the fun part: flipping the tarte tatin out of the pan and onto a plate. Grab a plate that is a bit bigger than the pan and place it upside down on top of the hot pan. Firmly press one hand onto the bottom of the plate and grip the handle of the pan with the other hand. In one smooth motion, maintaining the pressure of the plate onto the pan, flip the pan over, put the plate down, remove your hand from under the plate and lift off the pan. Voila! If everything went according to plan you should be looking at a saucy, golden disc of caramel, banana and pastry.

Cut the tart into four portions and serve straight away with a big dollop of vanilla bean ice cream.

This dish came about as a way of combining two ingredients that are plentiful as the weather starts to cool in the autumn months. The sweetness and acidity of the green tomatoes combines beautifully with a rich and creamy chestnut purée. Adorned with a lattice top, this pie may look traditional but it's sure to surprise with its not-so-traditional filling.

Green Tomato and Chestnut Pie

SERVES **8**

4 sheets of frozen shortcrust pastry, thawed

10 green Roma tomatoes, sliced

2 tablespoons plain flour

1 tablespoon raw sugar

Vanilla bean ice cream (see page 294), to serve

CHESTNUT PURÉE

500g fresh chestnuts, in shell

300ml full cream milk

½ vanilla pod, split, seeds scraped

55g (¼ cup) caster sugar

½ teaspoon ground cinnamon

½ teaspoon ground nutmeg

Preheat the oven to 220°C.

To shell the chestnuts, take a small knife and score an 'X' on the round bottom portion of each nut. Place the chestnuts on a baking tray in a small amount of water and bake for 10 minutes. Remove from the oven and set aside until cool enough to handle. Peel the shells off the nuts and discard.

Place the shelled nuts in a saucepan with the milk, vanilla seeds, sugar, cinnamon and nutmeg and let simmer for 10 minutes or until the nuts have softened. Smash the chestnuts using a potato masher and continue cooking on a low heat for 15–20 minutes, reducing the mixture until you have a thick purée. Remove from the heat and set aside to cool.

Put a lightly greased, 25cm pie dish out on the bench and place two of the pastry sheets over it, cutting them as needed to fit. Where the sheets overlap, brush a little water along the edge of the lower sheet and press the sheets together. Gently press the pastry into all the corners of the dish and then place in the fridge to rest for half an hour.

Preheat the oven to 180°C. Remove the dish from the fridge and trim off any excess dough.

Put the green tomatoes in a mixing bowl with the flour and mix it together. Spoon the chestnut purée into the pie base and then lay the tomatoes evenly on top.

Cut the remaining sheets of pastry into 2cm thick strips. To make the lattice, lay half of the strips over the pie dish making sure they are evenly spaced. Fold every second strip back on itself, so it only covers half the dish. Now this is where it gets a little tricky, though once you get the hang of it, it's as easy as pie! Starting on the centre line of the pie dish lay one of the remaining strips perpendicularly across the first lot. Unfold the folded strips over the perpendicular strip and then fold back the strips that weren't folded. Lay down another perpendicular strip, being sure to leave an even gap, and repeat the process until the lattice is complete. Trim any overhanging pastry and secure the lattice by crimping around the outside of the pie dish using your thumb and fore and middle fingers.

Sprinkle the raw sugar over the top and then bake in the oven for 30 minutes. The pie is cooked when the pastry on top is golden and the pastry on the bottom comes away from the dish. If the top is cooking a little quickly you can cover it with foil until the bottom is cooked.

Remove the pie from the oven and allow to cool a little in the dish. Slice into generous portions and serve with a scoop of homemade vanilla bean ice cream.

Hugh loves a fumble – a cross between a fool and a crumble, in which the crunchy topping is baked separately and sprinkled on at the last minute. One of his favourite versions uses plums, cooked briefly into a lovely, juicy compote. In the UK, he uses early season Victorias or Marjorie's Seedling but good Aussie varieties would be just-ripe Wilsons or Sugar plums.

Hugh's Spiced Plum Fumble

SERVES 4

INDEPENDENT CRUMBLE

225g (1½ cups) plain flour

½ teaspoon salt

200g cold, unsalted butter, cut into cubes

150g granulated or demerara sugar

100g ground almonds, medium oatmeal or porridge oats

SPICED PLUM COMPOTE

500g plums

50g (¼ cup) caster sugar, possibly a little more

1 star anise

A scrap of water

Natural yoghurt (see page 245), to serve

To make the independent crumble, first preheat the oven to 180°C. Put all the ingredients into a large bowl and rub them together with your fingertips until you have a crumbly dough. Squeeze the crumble mix in your hands to form clumps, then crumble these onto a large baking tray that has an edge. Spread out the lumpy crumble evenly.

Bake for about 25 minutes, giving the whole thing a good stir halfway through, until golden brown and crisp. Leave to cool completely, then transfer to an airtight container. You'll have more than you need for this recipe, but it stores well for a couple of weeks and can be used to top all sorts of fruity and/or creamy puds.

To make the plum compote, halve the plums and remove the stones. Put the fruit into a heavy-based pan with 50g sugar, the star anise and a little scrap of water – just enough to stop them catching. Heat them gently until the juices run, then simmer for 10 to 12 minutes, until the fruit is soft and pulpy (the skins will probably stay intact).

Let the compote start to cool, but taste while it is still warm enough to dissolve more sugar in it, should you need to. Add as much as you need to get the sweetness you like but leave it reasonably tart – remember that the crumble topping is pretty sweet. Leave the compote to cool completely. (If you have a glut of plums, make up a double or triple quantity of the compote. Keep it chilled in the fridge and eat it for breakfast with yoghurt and honey, or dish it up as a simple pud with a slice of plain sponge cake, or a brownie, and/or a scoop of ice cream.)

To serve, divide the plum compote between four serving plates. Add a couple of spoonfuls of yoghurt to one side of each plate, then sprinkle a handful of the crumble on the other side, or down the middle, and serve.

Pairing rhubarb and apple with a little zing of lemon means you have a perfect balance of sweet and sharp. Top with some pantry staples that create a crisp crust and you have an easy, warming winter pudding. All you need then is a dollop of good vanilla custard.

Apple and Rhubarb Crisp

SERVES 4

3 Granny Smith, Golden Delicious or Sundowner apples, peeled, cored, cut into chunky slices

2 rhubarb stalks, ends trimmed, cut into 3–4cm batons

Juice and zest of 1 lemon

1 tablespoon caster sugar

Vanilla custard (see page 291), to serve

CRISP TOPPING

60g unsalted butter, melted

100g (½ cup) brown sugar

60g (½ cup) rolled oats

½ teaspoon ground cinnamon

Preheat your oven to 190°C.

Pop the apple and rhubarb pieces in a mixing bowl with the lemon juice, lemon zest and caster sugar. Give everything a good mix and then arrange the fruit in the bottom of a baking dish.

To make the topping, combine the melted butter with the brown sugar, oats and cinnamon. Mix it together and then spoon it evenly over the fruit. Pop the baking dish in the oven and bake for around 45 minutes. It's ready when the fruit is soft and the oats are golden and crispy. Serve with a big spoonful of thick vanilla custard.

Everyone should know how to make a thick, velvety vanilla custard. Once you've mastered the technique – it's not that hard – you'll find yourself whipping it up all the time.

Vanilla Custard

MAKES ABOUT 500ML

250ml (1 cup) double cream

250ml (1 cup) full cream milk

1 vanilla pod, split, seeds scraped

6 free-range egg yolks

70g caster sugar

Combine the cream and milk in a heavy-based saucepan. Add the vanilla pod and seeds to the milk and cream and then gently heat the liquid until the surface just starts to let off wisps of steam.

While the cream and milk is heating, whisk together the egg yolks and sugar until pale and creamy.

Once the milk mixture is hot, pour one-third of it over the egg yolks while continually whisking. Once this is incorporated, continue whisking and pour over the remaining milk mixture.

Place the mixing bowl over a pot of gently simmering water, making sure that the bottom of the bowl doesn't touch the water. Gently stir with a wooden spoon until the custard has thickened and can coat the back of a spoon. Remove from the heat and enjoy straight away or cool and pop in the fridge, where it will keep for about a week.

I love making these molten-centred marvels, baked just long enough to form a decent crust. There are few things in the world more satisfying than driving a spoon into the warm pudding and having the whole thing collapse in a mess of chocolate sauce.

Gooey-centred Chocolate Puddings

SERVES **4**

120g unsalted butter, plus extra for greasing

Cocoa, for dusting

120g good-quality dark chocolate, roughly chopped

2 (whole) free-range eggs

2 free-range egg yolks

120g caster sugar

120g plain flour

Vanilla bean ice cream (see page 294), to serve

Preheat your oven to 200°C.

Butter the inside of four ramekins and then sprinkle them with some cocoa, turning the dishes as you do so, until the insides are lightly but evenly coated. Tap out any excess cocoa and place the ramekins to one side.

Combine the butter and chocolate together in a mixing bowl and place over a pot of simmering water to melt.

While that's happening, in a separate bowl whisk together the eggs, egg yolks and sugar until pale and thick. Then gradually pour in the melted chocolate and butter and whisk until well combined. Fold in the flour and then divide the mix among the ramekins.

Place the ramekins on an oven tray and slide it into the oven. Bake for 12 minutes, then remove from the oven and allow to stand for a couple of minutes.

Turn the puddings out onto serving plates and serve immediately with a scoop of vanilla bean ice cream.

Whether served with a warm and gooey chocolate pudding, a bowl of fruit or simply by itself, homemade vanilla ice cream is easy to make and infinitely more delicious and creamy than anything you can buy in the shops.

Vanilla Bean Ice Cream

MAKES 500ml

375ml (1½ cups) full cream milk

375ml (1½ cups) double cream

2 vanilla pods, split, seeds scraped

150g caster sugar

8 free-range egg yolks

Combine the milk, cream and the vanilla pods and seeds in a saucepan on a medium heat and bring to a simmer.

While the liquid is heating, whisk together the sugar and egg yolks until pale and thick. Pour the warm vanilla milk through a strainer into a jug, and then add it to the yolk mixture while stirring constantly.

Return the mixture to the saucepan and gently cook until it is thick enough to coat the back of a spoon. Strain through a fine strainer once again, then leave to cool to room temperature.

Pour the cooled mixture into an ice cream maker and churn until smooth and firm.

If you don't have an ice cream churner, don't despair – you can still make creamy ice cream by hand. Once you've made your custard base, pour it into a sturdy, deep-sided tray and place it, uncovered, in a freezer. After an hour pull the tray out and check – if the mix has started to freeze around the edges, beat the mixture well with a spatula or a strong whisk. To get a smooth ice cream you need to stop any large crystals forming, so repeat the process every half an hour or so. After about 3 hours you'll have handmade, velvety ice cream.

There is something deeply satisfying about a fragrant, creamy bowl of sweetened rice on a cold winter's night. I would go as far as to say that a simple rice pudding is the ultimate comfort food for those of us with a sweet tooth. It's also one of the easiest of all puddings, a one-pot dish using pantry staples that is my go-to dessert when I have no dessert. Add some syrupy, poached fruits and you're in business.

Rice Pudding

SERVES 4

220g (1 cup) short grain rice, like Arborio or Carnaroli

25g unsalted butter

750ml (3 cups) full cream milk

80g (⅓ cup) caster sugar

1 vanilla pod, split, seeds scraped

180ml (¾ cup) double cream

Place the rice, butter, milk, sugar and vanilla seeds and pod in a saucepan over a medium heat and bring gently to a simmer. Reduce the heat to low and cook for 25–30 minutes, stirring occasionally, until rice is tender but still al dente.

Stir the cream into the rice pudding, then spoon into bowls.

Serve warm with syrupy, poached fruits or a saucy spoonful of baked rhubarb or roast quinces (see page 298).

Quinces rarely grace the shelves of a supermarket, perhaps because they are inedible in their natural state. However, these cousins of the apple are well worth searching out when they're in season. With a long, gentle cook the hard, white flesh of the quince becomes yielding and flushes a beautiful ruby colour. Some varieties will turn a deep red and others orange, so don't stress too much about the colour – that spicy, aromatic flavour is the important part.

Roast Quinces

SERVES 4

60g (⅓ cup) brown sugar

Zest and juice of 2 oranges

1 vanilla pod, split, seeds scraped

3 cloves

2 quinces, peeled, cored, cut into 8 slices lengthways

Preheat your oven to 150°C.

Put the sugar, orange juice, orange zest, vanilla pod and seeds and cloves in a small mixing bowl and whisk with a fork to combine.

Spread the quince in a single layer in a deep-sided baking tray and pour over the orange juice mix. Give the fruit a quick toss to evenly coat it in the liquid. Tightly cover the tray with a sheet of foil and then pop it in the oven for at least 2 hours. Every now and then, take the tray out and baste the quince with the cooking syrup and cover again. When the quince is cooked it will be a deep, rich orange or red.

Serve with a generous spoonful of natural yoghurt (see page 245) or spoon the fruit over a creamy rice pudding (see page 297).

Quinces are very high in pectin, which makes them the perfect candidate for turning into a fruit cheese. Quince cheese, or membrillo as the Spanish call it, is like a cross between a jelly and a very thick paste. You can cut it into slabs and serve with firm, bitey cheeses as part of a cheese platter, or add a spoonful to enliven a slow-cooked winter stew.

Quince Cheese

MAKES ABOUT 1KG

2kg quinces, peeled, cored, cut into 2–3cm pieces (keep the core and peel)

Water, as needed

About 1.2kg caster sugar

Wrap the core and peel in a little muslin-cloth pouch and seal it with some twine.

Put the quince pieces, the muslin and peel bag and just enough cold water to cover everything in a heavy-based saucepan. Pop a lid on, bring it to a gentle simmer, then continue cooking for about an hour, or until the fruit is very tender. Leave it to stand for a couple of hours.

Discard the muslin bag and pass the cooked fruit through a sieve or a mouli. Weigh the purée and then return it to the pan and add an equal weight of sugar. Stir well and cook this, uncovered, for around 1 hour on a very low heat. You'll know that it's done if a wooden spoon trailed through the pot leaves a path that holds its shape for a couple of seconds.

Line a low-sided tray with baking paper and pour the cooked quince on top. Let the mixture level out, then lay another sheet of baking paper on top and pop it into the fridge to set.

To store, wrap the cheese in baking paper and then wrap again in cling film. Stored this way the quince cheese should last until next year's quince season.

I love a good jam. Slathered onto a piece of toast with loads of butter or baked into a tray of delicious jam drops, the sweet fruity flavour really is a special treat. You can make jam out of pretty much any fruit and even the odd vegetable. Rhubarb jam is a particular favourite of mine because of its unique flavour and aroma and its vibrant crimson colour. Rhubarb is very low in pectin and doesn't make a fantastic jam on its own, so I've added a little pectin here to help the setting process.

Rhubarb Jam

1kg rhubarb, cut into 3cm batons

1kg caster sugar

Zest and juice of 1 lemon

8g of pectin

Place two small plates in the freezer – these will be used later to check if the jam has reached its setting point.

Put three-quarters of the rhubarb and all of the sugar in a heavy-based saucepan and gently heat, stirring occasionally, until the sugar has melted. Add the zest and juice of the lemon as well as the pectin and increase the heat so that the jam is on a gentle boil. Use a spoon to skim off any scum that comes to the surface.

Continue boiling the jam for around 10 minutes, and then remove one of the plates from the freezer and spoon a small amount of jam onto it. After a minute, push the jam with the tip of your finger – if it has firmed and wrinkles when pushed, then the jam is ready to go. If the jam is still runny, boil for another 5–10 minutes and then check again.

When the jam has reached its setting point, pop the rest of the rhubarb into the jam, remove from the heat and allow to cool a little. The residual heat of the jam will cook the rhubarb and leave you with a lovely chunky jam.

Transfer into sterilised jars (see page 23), pop the lids on and allow to cool completely before storing. The jam will keep in a cool, dark pantry for six months.

The tangy golden flesh of the tamarillo, aka the tree tomato, is a great way to wake up your taste buds first thing in the morning. In mid autumn, when they start to ripen, I like to scoop out the flesh and spread it on a slice of toast with a sprinkle of raw sugar. Or if I'm feeling particularly fancy, I'll poach them in a sweet syrup and serve them with a stack of pancakes.

Pancakes with Poached Tamarillos

SERVES 4

PANCAKES

300g (2 cups) plain flour

2 teaspoons baking powder

1 teaspoon salt

2 free-range eggs

700ml full cream milk

30g unsalted butter, plus extra for frying

Lightly whipped pure cream, to serve

POACHED TAMARILLOS

4 ripe tamarillos, score a small cross on the base of each

1 vanilla pod, split, seeds scraped

55g (¼ cup) caster sugar

250ml (1 cup) water

3 tablespoons honey

Sift the flour, baking powder and salt together into a mixing bowl. Make a well in the centre, crack the eggs into it and then pour in the milk. Gently whisk to make the batter then cover the bowl and leave to stand for an hour.

While the batter is resting, bring a medium saucepan full of water to the boil and have a bowl of iced water at the ready. Pop the tamarillos in the boiling water for about 30 seconds. Remove them from the pot and cool in the iced water, then peel off the skins and cut into 1cm-thick rounds.

Put the vanilla pod and seeds into a saucepan along with the sugar, the water and the honey. Gently bring to a simmer and let it bubble away for 5 minutes to reduce a little. Add the tamarillo slices, simmer for a further 2 minutes or so, and then remove from the heat. Leave the fruit to cool and infuse with the syrup.

Heat a low-sided frypan over a medium heat and add the 30g of butter. When it melts pour it into the pancake batter and fold it through. Increase the heat in the pan a little and add a knob of butter. Once the butter is bubbling, pour in enough pancake batter to cover the base of the pan. Cook until little bubbles start to appear and then flip the pancake, cooking on the other side until cooked through. Transfer the cooked pancake to a warm plate and repeat until there's no batter left.

Divide the pancakes among four plates and spoon the tamarillos and syrup over the top. Spoon over some whipped cream – and tuck in.

Though commonly available as a commercial fruit, wild cultivars of finger lime can still be found around the New South Wales and Queensland border. The long, cylindrical fruit adorn the spiky bushes from summer through to autumn and come in a variety of colours.

Widely known for the globulous pulp that is like a citrus caviar, finger limes lend a tang to seafood and salads and a refreshing kick to cold drinks. (For a change from the 'ol lemon-squeeze over an oyster, try a teaspoonful of finger-lime pulp.) To preserve the harvest so that it can be enjoyed year round, I like to knock together a little finger lime cordial. Even though I plan to keep it, I usually end up enjoying it with soda, gin and mint as a refreshing summer tipple.

Sweet and Tangy Finger Lime Cordial

MAKES 650ML

Note: Start this the day before you want to use the cordial, as it must be left overnight.

CORDIAL

500ml (2 cups) water

500g caster sugar

150ml white wine vinegar

6 finger limes, washed and pricked with a fork

FOR FOUR DRINKS

Ice

Small bunch of mint

240ml finger lime cordial

An optional splash of gin

1 litre soda water

To make the cordial, pour the water, sugar and vinegar into a saucepan, stir, and bring the liquid to the boil to dissolve the sugar.

Remove the syrup from the heat and add the finger limes. Allow the fruit to steep in the syrup overnight to impart its flavour, then strain the liquid into a sterilised bottle (see page 23). You can use this straight away, or pop it in the pantry and use it within a couple of months.

To make a refreshing drink, add the ice, mint, cordial and gin to a glass jug and then pour over the soda water. Give it a good mix with a spoon or a straw, pour into tumblers and then retreat to a shady verandah.

After working in the garden on a blasting hot, midsummer day, there is nothing better in the world than a big cup of sweet and icy watermelon granita. It's a breeze to make and is a summer treat that I look forward to every year.

Watermelon Granita

SERVES 4

185ml (¾ cup) water

170g (¾ cup) caster sugar

Small handful of mint leaves

2kg watermelon, rind and seeds removed

Place a couple of rimmed baking trays in the freezer to chill.

Combine the water and sugar in a saucepan and heat gently until the sugar has dissolved. Remove from the heat and throw in the mint leaves to infuse. Leave the syrup to cool, then remove and discard the leaves.

When the sugar syrup is completely cool, purée the watermelon using a food processor and then combine with the syrup.

Pour the watermelon liquid into the cold baking trays and put them in the freezer to set for 2 hours. By then the granita will be partially frozen. Use a fork to break apart any crystals that have formed and then return the trays to the freezer. Repeat this process every 30 minutes or so until you have a texture like sparkling pink snow.

To serve, scoop the granita into a chilled cup, then eat it with a teaspoon in a nice shady spot.

These lassis are great to whip up to serve as a refreshing drink after a spicy curry. They're thick, sweet and minty, and almost a meal in themselves.

Sweet Mint Lassi

SERVES 4

Small bunch of mint, leaves picked

750ml (3 cups) natural yoghurt (see page 245)

375ml (1½ cups) full cream milk

2 tablespoons honey

A few pinches of crushed pistachios

Combine the mint leaves, yoghurt, milk and honey in a blender and give it a good whizz. Pour into four glasses and top each with a pinch of crushed pistachios.

ACKNOWLEDGEMENTS

First and foremost I would like to thank my beautiful partner Alicia, who by the time this book is published will be nursing our first child. Without your unwavering support and eternal patience I would've had a nervous breakdown. I promise that next time we go on a holiday I won't spend the whole time feverishly hunched over a keyboard! Love you Leesh.

I would also like to extend my eternal gratitude to Hugh and the team at Keo films. It seems like only yesterday that I was just a bloke living in Tassie, cooking and gardening. I thank you all for giving me the opportunity to share my passion with a wider audience and giving me the confidence to believe that I could actually pull the whole television-presenter thing off. It's been an interesting couple of years, to say the least, and I'm looking forward to continuing the adventure into the future.

Massive thanks to Natalie Bellos and Xa Shaw Stewart at Bloomsbury Publishing in London – you have both been incredibly supportive, patient and upbeat throughout this entire process. Your professionalism has been inspirational, and without both of your input, this book would be a mere shadow of its final, beautiful self. I'll never forget the two of you taking me to a flash cocktail bar while I was in London; if you're ever in Tilba, it's my shout at the Drom.

A big thanks to the enthusiastic team at Bloomsbury Publishing in Sydney – you have treated Alicia and me like family since the beginning and I can't wait to work with you all well into the future.

Thanks to Antony Topping for easing me into the world of publishing. You've been incredibly supportive throughout the entire process and I truly appreciate your guidance.

A *huge* thanks to Eugenie Baulch. When this whole thing started I had no idea how a book was put together. I now know that it is through the relentless hard work of talented folk such as yourself. Thank you so much for your positivity and patience after innumerable late replies to emails and long periods of radio silence. I'm a tough bloke to get hold of at the best of times, let alone when there's a deadline involved. Thanks too to Margaret Barca for her thorough copyediting and deciphering of my ramblings.

Thanks to Mark Chew for the dazzling photography. I knew that you were going to smash it when you first pulled out that war-battered old Canon of yours. You captured the peace and the beauty of the farm with a deft touch, and the food looks *amazing*! Thank you to Kat Chadwick for your fun-filled illustrations, which have really brought the pages of the book to life.

Thank you Trisha for sharing your dazzling design talents and welcoming me into your home with gifts of espresso, sparkling tap water and wine. Thank you Tessa for your beautiful attention to detail when styling the props on the food and farm shoots – I'm wearing a lurid collared shirt with short sleeves just for you.

Thank you to Deb and Emma for all your hard work with the cook shoots and helping to iron out any last-minute kinks in the recipes.

Finally a big thank you to all the crew that have worked on *River Cottage Australia*, past and present. I'm just the boofhead on camera, and without the rest of you none of this would have been possible.

DIRECTORY

HAND TOOLS FOR THE VEGGIE GARDEN

Allsun Farm, Gundaroo, offer an incredible selection of quality tools for taming the veggie patch:
allsun.com.au

KITCHEN EQUIPMENT

These suppliers have an extensive selection of quality hand-cranked tools for making sausages or passata:

Butcher at Home
butcherathome.com.au

Orange Farm Hardware
orangefarmhardware.com.au

FLOUR SUPPLIERS

These Australian mills produce organic grains:

Four Leaf Milling
fourleafmilling.com.au

Kialla Pure Foods
kiallafoods.com.au

FISHING

For details about licensing requirements, bag limits and protected species refer to the relevant State fisheries sites:

NSW dpi.nsw.gov.au
VIC depi.vic.gov.au
QLD daff.gov.au
SA pir.sa.gov.au
WA fish.wa.gov.au
TAS sea fishery dpipe.tas.gov.au
TAS inland fishery ifs.tas.gov.au
ACT environment.act.gov.au
NT nt.gov.au

If you're headed to your local fish market and you want to know a little about the sustainability of what's on offer, refer to the Australian Marine Conservation Society's excellent website or phone app. There is information about the sustainability of around 90 seafood species, simply laid out to help you make an informed choice.
sustainableseafood.org.au

INDEX

First published in Great Britain 2015

Bloomsbury Australia
Level 4, 387 George St
Sydney 2000 NSW
Australia

Bloomsbury Publishing Plc
50 Bedford Square
London
WC1B 3DP

bloomsbury.com

Bloomsbury is a trademark of Bloomsbury Publishing Plc

Bloomsbury Publishing, Sydney, London,
New Delhi and New York

A CIP catalogue record for this book is available from
the British Library

ISBN 978 1 4088 5838 7

Project editor: Eugenie Baulch
Designer: Trisha Garner, DesignPatsy
Photographer: Mark Chew
Food stylist: Deb Kaloper
Prop stylist: Tessa Kavanagh
Illustrator: Kat Chadwick
Copyeditor: Margaret Barca
Indexer: Penny Mansley

10 9 8 7 6 5 4 3 2 1

Printed and bound in China by C&C Offset Printing Co Ltd